FLEETING THOUGHTS
by
MICHAEL McGAN

Copyright © 1997, 2001 by Michael McGan
All rights reserved.
No part of this book may be reproduced, stored in a retrieval system, or transmitted by any means, electronic, mechanical, photocopying, recording, or otherwise, without written permission from the author.

ISBN: 0-75962-846-7

This book is printed on acid free paper.

1stBooks – rev. 9/26/01

For Betty and Howard

Thanks to Sandy, Lisa, Joy, Bill, Lara, Tim, Dan, Annie, Lori, Heather, Terry and Darryl.

Special thanks to Sharon Baker for editing, and Kelly Devall for the cover.

Fleeting Thoughts

POUR THE RUM SLOWLY

Have you ever dreamed of the perfect vacation? The vacation where you lie under a palm tree sipping pina coladas on some tropical beach while Caribbean music drifts by on the sea breeze? And let's not forget the most important part of the dream, the part where this can all fall into place for a reasonable price. Have you ever dreamed this? Well, so did my wife and I. We decided to make it a reality. We were going to Jamaica. Mostly because of that last part of the dream. And it went like this.

We descended into the Jamaican airport late one afternoon, through heavy clouds, which we had not seen all day. This had a negative affect on my wife, in that she began to frown and say things like "Great! Isn't this just our luck? Bright sunshine all day from Albany to Miami, and here we are about to be rained on." When it rains, it pours.

Walking through the airport we encountered a group of people brightly dressed in colorful floral prints and singing "Welcome to Jamaica", a tune where if you changed the lyrics, it sounded exactly like "On Top of Old Smokey". This stood right out to me, being a music lover and all, and what also stood right out to me was that none of these people were smiling. Granted it was probably their twenty-fifth time through that song today at the rate of incoming planes, but they could have at least pretended to mean it. They weren't making me feel all warm and fuzzy. After going through customs and grabbing our luggage we stopped at the desk displaying the logo of our resort. A smiling Jamaican man asked our names and then began to glance at his clipboard. Then it came.

"I'm sorry. Your resort has been overbooked. We're going to put you up someplace else tonight, tomorrow you can go to your resort." My response, despite the spontaneity, was none the less brilliant. "What?" And then I added "This is bullstuff!" My wife was not as easygoing about the situation. She began to tell this still smiling man, that we had planned this trip well in advance, that everything had been arranged by our travel agent and that we wanted to stay in the resort that we had paid good money to stay in. This was all laced with colorful expletives due to frustration as the smiling resort representative held his position. His position was that we were now in a foreign country and unless we wanted to sleep in the airport, we would go along with his plan for our accommodations.

I demanded to speak to the resort manager. I was handed the telephone and spoke to a woman who I could barely hear as my wife tried calling our travel agent to no avail. All of the pay phones were out of order. The bottom line seemed to be that we were not going where we had planned to be this evening. My wife returned from the pay phones and demanded to see the clipboard that this still smiling man kept referring to and glancing at. He was not going to let her see that.

So smoothly changing her strategy she commenced to try and rip it out of his hands. At this point he stopped smiling. Also at this point I took hold of my wife and reminded her that we weren't in Kansas anymore so to speak, and that we should probably just go with the flow, as all of our fellow vacationers of all races, creeds and nationalities had departed for their destinations, leaving my wife and I with about ten surly looking Jamaican airport employees and taxi drivers. Checkmate.

Walking outside our "shuttle bus" was now a small car and the driver who had been observing the events inside wasted no time in trying to diffuse the situation. He took me aside and asked me if I like to party and then began to offer me a wide range of "party favors". All very much illegal I might add. I declined and told him that the only thing I wanted was to arrive at our hotel. "No problem, mon." He took us to our substitute hotel for the night which didn't turn out to be too bad, but it wasn't where we were supposed to be. We went down to the dining area which was right by the ocean and had something to eat. So did the little scrawny cats that the sign said not to feed. I couldn't resist throwing them a few little pieces of sirloin and fish from my plate when nobody was looking.

Hey, I didn't ask to be eating at a hotel with starving, demented cats rubbing my leg.

Later that night in an attempt to relax and unwind, we checked out a sea-side bar down the road. "Two for one Coronas starting at nine o'clock" said someone over the PA system. I walked up and ordered two Coronas. I was charged for two Coronas. I said, "Hey man (mon), I thought it was two for one."

He said "Yeah mon, at nine."

I said "It *is* nine."

He said "No mon, it's eight." At this point in time, whatever it was, I became very confused and decided that I should seek help. I did so by asking a nearby couple for the *correct* time. "They didn't let you know either, huh?" They went on to tell us what the airline had failed to tell us: There was an hour difference in time down here. What's up with that?

Well, at least this explained our arrival being an hour late. I set my watch back and said, "I don't even like Corona." Oh well, we settled in and chatted with our new aquaintences who were from Boston. He was a cop. I considered asking him to arrest the manager of the hotel we were supposed to be at, the guy at the airport, and possibly the bartender for charging me eight tokens for two beers despite the fact I had no idea what time it was. I let it go, besides, a Boston cop would probably be out of his jurisdiction down here.

Later, we danced to throbbing club music until it was time for our taxi driver to pick us up. He was there at the door and escorted us out through a gauntlet of "salesmen". He drove us safely back to our hotel, although he was on the wrong side of the road the whole way, at least from my skewed perspective. What did I know at this point? The entire day had been weird. We were beyond tired. It was time for this long, crazy day to come to an end.

The next morning after breakfast with the cats, we got a taxi to our original destination, where we had to sit in the lobby while our reservations were reviewed. There was another problem now. One of the vouchers for the last two days of our stay was missing. We suspected the guy at the airport may have kept it. Then we suspected that our travel agent had failed to put it in our packet. We also suspected that we were missing a gorgeous day on a gorgeous beach, and asked the manager if there was a room where we could change into our swimwear to get outside while they sorted everything out. She obliged, we were soon soaking up the sun by the ocean. At two o'clock we were officially in, got our wristbands, and started soaking up tropical drinks by the pool.

It all pretty much got better by this point. I got involved in reggae dance lessons in front of about a hundred people pool side. In the lesson group, which included my wife, I was fine. But then we had to dance across the stage, one by one, showing the moves that we had learned, or in my case, failed to learn. So this was not an easy thing for me to do. Despite this, the crowd cheered me on and I made it through an experience that back home, completely sober, would have put me in therapy for years.

My wife got her hair braided at the salon. She looked better than a "10". Later, we took a glass-bottom boat ride which was pretty lame, except for when my wife asked the driver why the glass was all scratched and he said "sharks". That was pretty funny and even he laughed. The biggest fish we saw was smaller than a scrawny cat. The coral was in bad shape, probably because of glass-bottom boats or something, but the water was a beautiful shade of turquoise and very warm.

I joined the pool volleyball teams which included some Jamaican staff. When it was my turn to serve, because of my shaved head, one of the Jamaicans on the other team was calling me "Captain Picard". Everyone laughed including myself. Then I smoked them for three points in a row. After about an hour in the pool I realized that I was wearing my favorite watch. It was not waterproof. I tried to revive it but it was not to be. It passed away around 4:15 pm. Afterwards I was a bit of a pool side celebrity. The guys would see me, smile and yell "Picard!" It was cool. There was also two guys that looked exactly like Chris Farely, and Jeanne-Claude Van Dam. Celebrity look-alike week I guess.

The Jamaican staff at the resort were great. They were very friendly and went out of their way to make you feel comfortable. One night, we dined with a couple from South Dakota who had just gotten married. He was a highly bleached-blonde white guy and she was a black woman with long braided hair.

Fleeting Thoughts

They were a striking couple, both hairdressers. They seemed a little stressed with the pressures of the marriage/honeymoon vacation thing. They were exhausted. They took some great shots of my wife and I on the beach at sunset, we did the same for them.

Tourists, mostly Americans, of all colors and ethnic backgrounds were getting along great, relaxing, having a good time together, vacationing. And in the end, we all came away and went home with the same feelings. We were really sick of pounding club-mix reggae music, being propositioned for taxis and other things, and let's not forget, being rubbed on during dinner by skanky little cats. In spite of these things Jamaica was really cool and the people were great. So overall, it's all good, mon.

Michael McGan

ALL KEYED UP

My wife and I recently drove out of Miami and down US-1 to the Florida Keys. Some people might say that this ride is boring, but when it's early spring and you're from upstate New York, US-1 looks like the highway to heaven. The most peculiar thing about Florida is that it is so flat. There are no mountains on the horizon. This flatness is believed to be from intensive tourism over the centuries, the trudging of the sunburned, flip-flopped masses over the highlands, reducing the mountain ranges to mere speed-bumps.

On US-1, the ocean is a stone's throw away on either side of you for much of the journey and it's only slightly lower than the road. If you really wanted to, you could go off the road onto one of the little pathways and in seconds drive your car right into the ocean! Wouldn't that be something the whole family would talk about for years to come! Well, I decided against that, and it's probably best because it was a rental car, you know how those people can be.

It was about seven-thirty in the evening and the sun was brilliant red, melting into the ocean like...like... (I'm at a loss for metaphor here. Please fill in your own.) Very nice! It was just like that. I started to go a little faster thinking we might be able to watch the sunset from my brother-in-law's house, but then I remembered that his house faces due south. On a

Fleeting Thoughts

clear day, with a very powerful telescope, you might be able to see a land full of classic American cars from the fifties and sixties. But right now, we were seeing an amazing sunset on the Gulf side of US-1. An hour later we arrived, unpacked and settled in for a few days of the Keys.

Our first adventure involved "tubing" out on the high seas. Here's a tip - don't go with the kneeling position. Here's another tip - keep the squirming to a minimum as you try to find a position that will reduce the relentless pounding that your body's private areas are taking. Final tip - don't try to change positions while flying along, bouncing over waves while everyone in the boat is looking back at your grimacing face, laughing hysterically. This will send you tumbling into the drink at high speeds, and leave you there bobbing in the warm water, thinking about all the large toothy fish that like warm ocean water, and how the parts of your body that are below the surface have already been thoroughly tenderized.

Minutes later there were fins in the water, honestly. Lucky for me, it was a "pod" of dolphins. We slowed to let them pass in front of us. My brother-in-law, being very knowledgeable in all things "marine", guessed that the large and bloated one was probably close to giving birth because they were staying near the surface, heading into a bay. How can dolphins tell when their water breaks? We didn't stick around for the cigars, but I'm sure that it went just fine.

Later, we went to one of the Florida Key's last historic treasures, "The No Name Pub". It started out as a general store but business was apparently so good that in the late 1930's, they decided to put a brothel upstairs. "Yes, I'd like ten pounds of flour, a dozen eggs, and a couple of hookers." In the 1940's, they closed the brothel and replaced it with a bait and tackle shop. Talk about being fickle. In the 1950's the restaurant was added. Their motto is "Great Food-Lousy Service". I want to tell you, I was a little disappointed in that the service was very good. So was their pizza. We signed a dollar bill and stapled it on the wall, which is what you do there to become part of history. It's a small restaurant, but if they expand a few times the owners could quite possibly take an early retirement on the wallpaper alone.

Another memorable excursion took us to one of the thousands of small deserted islands, or keys that are almost entirely covered by mangroves. Mangroves are apparently large green water loving plants, that spread more quickly than rumors of increased taxes. This particular key is a secret of the locals. (For a small fee, I won't reveal it's location. Cash, checks, or money orders are all cool.) When the tide goes out into the Gulf of Mexico the white sand beach surrounding the tiny island becomes huge. People bring barbecue grills, chairs, coolers, their dogs, etc… and make a day of it. Here it is important to pack up before the tide comes back in and the island once again becomes tiny.

Fleeting Thoughts

We were the first ones to arrive there on this particular day, so we were totally alone, miles out into the ocean. The only sound you could hear was my camera clicking and an occasional belch from all the Pepsi I had consumed. My nephew and niece were making a sand castle and my brother-in-law was telling us how tricky it is to get in because of the shallows, without running your boat aground, when only minutes later, that's exactly what happened to the next arrival. They all got out of the boat to make it more buoyant. This did the trick of releasing the boat from the sandy bottom. They pulled their boat in and at that point I felt what people of many lands have felt through the ages: "Get lost! Go discover your own piece of Paradise!" But you can't be that way. Everybody was friendly and by this point the island was getting pretty big. When we left there was only a total of five boats there, hardly a situation of overcrowding.

Key West at sundown is the "happening" place to be while in the Florida Keys. I was standing on the pier at Mallory Square sipping a pina colada, while watching the "Cat Man" try to get some scruffy feline to jump through a flaming hoop, and I thought, "You just can't get this kind of high quality entertainment back where we come from". My brother-in-law, who is in law enforcement, turned to me and with a cynical grin he said, "This must be violating some kind of animal cruelty laws." I agreed, but what do I know from the Keys? I'm from upstate New York.

Michael McGan

Every time the "Cat Man" would turn his back the cat would jump down from it's platform and start walking aimlessly around in typical Key West fashion.

The "Cat Man" was getting a little frustrated and casting furtive glances at his empty hat, the one he hoped would be filled with cash after the show. That's how people make money in Key West, so if you go off to find gainful employment down there, the first thing you must do is go to a circus and figure out what category you fall into. This will be based on your personal strengths. You may decide you want to be a trapeze artist, a lion tamer, a human cannonball, etc. Then you must perfect your act, sort of. Or at least scale it down a bit. For example, instead of working with real terrifying lions, you are in fact working with real, terrified domestic house cats. Next you must buy a hat that is at least six sizes bigger than your actual head, and place it on the ground in front of the area where you are performing. You are now on your way to financial independence.

But getting back to the "Cat Man", the stubborn cat would not make the jump so the show was officially over. Personally, I say Good for the cat, man! The crowd gave the guy a big hand anyway and he probably did alright as far as money. But we wondered about the poor cat that wouldn't make the jump. I told my brother-in-law that he should buy a bigger bag of cat food. He might have another stray

Fleeting Thoughts

wandering his way from the side of the road along US-1. We walked around as the sunset commenced.

There was a family doing all sorts of circus type performances. They were actually pretty good. They had a young boy riding a unicycle while playing the bag pipes... no that was another guy... I don't remember, but he was riding a unicycle and doing something equally impressive at the same time. My brother-in-law turned to me and with a cynical grin said, "This must be against some kind of child labor laws." They asked for a volunteer from the audience to come out and juggle. My wife, ever the showgirl, went out there and got a big hand from the crowd because she is in fact a "fair" juggler and managed to juggle three balls for around ten seconds. Not bad.

My nephew and niece, following their aunt's example eagerly volunteered to try the hoola-hoop. Being there with young kids, this act was good family entertainment unlike some of the other shows that had performers insulting individual crowd members, spewing sexual entendres, and pathetic hints that other things could be substituted for money in the hats.

Soon the circus show was over and that hat was being filled. The father or "ring leader", or whatever, was actually a really nice guy who looked like a young David Crosby. After the show he took the time to get the kids spinning those hoola-hoops so we could snap a few pictures. And because the young boy that was part of the act had performed flawlessly,

Michael McGan

there was no anxiety as to what would happen to *him* after the show.

The weirdest entertainers were the ones posing as statues. They'd stand there motionless, painted all white like they were marbleized until they felt that onlookers were thoroughly impressed, then with the slightest motion, they would extend an upturned palm, snatch the cash from the outreached hand of some way too generous and easily impressed tourist. With uncanny speed, they stowed it somewhere on their statue-like person, then return to their original pose. Get out of here! Get a real job, you posers! We walked around a bit in town. My brother-in-law at one point turned to me, and with a cynical grin, he said "Look at these people. I'll probably be arresting half of them tomorrow."

We passed "Sloppy Joe's" but decided that with the kids along, sitting inside, getting sloppy and discussing Hemingway probably wasn't a good idea. So we called it a night and headed out of town as mo-peds flew by us dodging, weaving through traffic, running red lights, and generally driving like deranged tourists who have little or no experience riding a mo-ped. They had no idea where they were going but want to get there using maximum speed and a minimum amount of brain cells. My brother-in-law turned to me and with a cynical grin said "You haven't had the complete Key West experience until you've seen a mo-ped fatality. At first I'd feel real bad about it, but after a while... They'll rent them to

Fleeting Thoughts

anyone. There are accidents every night. My partner and I had one run right into the front of our truck a couple of weeks ago. Drunk, flyin' along, he ran a red light. Crashed right into us! Pulled him out from under the truck. He was a mess. It's just beautiful down here."

When the day of our departure came we started it the same way we had started every other day down here refreshed and warm, opposed to stressed and chilled. We sat with coffee and muffins on the front porch overlooking the ocean. My brother-in-law looked out at the brilliant, turquoise water, and without a trace of cynicism, he grinned and said, "Another beautiful day in Paradise."

We were driving up US-1 to Miami and our flight home, tanned, relaxed, and I was thinking: I need to bring this car back with a full tank of gas. So I stopped in Key Largo and filled it up. When we got to the rental place near the airport I parked it. This guy comes out of nowhere with some kind of device, points it at the car, gets his reading and says, "You're going to have to pay twelve dollars for gas because you didn't bring it back full." He never looked at the gas gauge.

"I just filled it up like an hour ago. Cost me eighteen dollars! What are you talkin' about?" He walked briskly off to scan some other cars with his high-tech gas detecting apparatus. I checked the gas gauge again and it was a hair below the full line. If you looked at it from the right angle, you'd say it was full. At least I would, anyway. It was probably a gallon or two off. So how much is gas in Miami? Six dollars a gallon? I could have drivin this car right into the friggin' ocean, but did I? No. That's gratitude for you. "Don't worry...be happy". Yeah, right.

My wife stormed inside to match wits and wills with the ungrateful rental car people while I secured our luggage. She came out weary, but victorious. Soon we were waiting for late flights actually running to catch connecting flights, riding shuttles, and finally in the end, losing our luggage. I miss paradise.

Fleeting Thoughts

THIS WEEK'S SOAPY UPDATES

They're Not My Children: Todd and Glenda went spelunking only to discover a crazy old woman who has been living in the cave for years. As it turns out, it's Todd's mother Edna. She tells him that she came to the cave to escape "the little people" who were sneaking into her room at night and playing canasta. Franky proposes to Sarah at a wrestling event, only to be killed when an enormous man is hurled out of the ring, crushing him. Sarah is overtaken with grief but forgives "El Gordo, the Human Behemoth." After Franky is taken away Sarah and El Gordo embrace and make plans for the weekend. Bill finds Bob with Nell. Bill and Bob get into a fight. Nell tries to break it up by firing shots in the air. One of the shots hits the chain holding a large expensive chandelier, which falls striking Bill on the head and rendering him unconscious. When he comes to he thinks he is Willie Wonka. Mary Jo wonders how to tell Lance that Lance Jr. is really the baby of "Bugsy", the pest control man. Lance is concerned about the baby having three eyes and two noses, but takes comfort in the fact that it wasn't twins.

Some Other World: During a Fresh Whiff award dinner, honoring Eddie for highest deodorant sales, twins, Lori and Loona switch rolls. Who is the crescent, and who is the snowflake? Only Lloyd is not fooled. But when they return together from the restroom and desert is served, neither wants coffee and Lloyd begins to panic. Tiffany catches William flirting with Tina and slaps him. William slaps Tina. Tina slaps the waiter who resembles Gus, soon there is a brawl. At the hospital Patty comes out of her coma and claims to be Queen of England. She fingers Stewart as the one who bopped her over the head with a truncheon nine years ago. Margo disappears from her prison cell in a puff of smoke, then reappears in Paris during a magic show at the Bastille. Tanya, Margo's sister who also happens to be in France at the time, is swept out to sea after Jonathan slips her a "Mickey". She falls asleep on her float as the tide takes her out. She is rescued by a Norwegian fishing boat off the coast of Finland.

While The World Burns: Felicia falls off a bar stool striking her head and loses her memory. Rick, a complete stranger convinces her that he is her husband and takes her to the Poconos. Once there she tells Rick that she has been planning to leave him and join a religious cult led by a man named "Chuck" who she met by the pool. Felicia is drawn by his teachings about money being an unnecessary burden, until it comes time at one of his lectures to order some take out. It is here that Felicia and the rest of Chuck's hungry followers awaken from their trance, and rush the stage. In the ensuing melee the podium falls on Felicia's head and she gets her memory back, but not her money. Marty, who as it turns out has no twin,

Fleeting Thoughts

drives by as Felicia is hitchhiking back home. He pulls the beer truck over to pick her up. Felicia believes this must be a true religious experience because of her fondness for beer and all. She begins to weep.

Misguiding Lights: Brooke is devastated when she learns that Sonny is not really a Wall Street wiz but a struggling hot dog vender with delusions of grandeur. But he charms her anyway with his sweet relish and they run off to get married before Hank gets back from the gun show. Ray's hair transplant goes terribly wrong. When Nikki sees him she faints and falls out the open window. She is rushed to the hospital where she is now in a coma. (Do you see recurring themes here?) Vernon hears a song that he wrote on the radio and gets excited until he realizes that it's Charles singing. Charles is (you guessed it) his evil twin, and the one with the better voice. Harriet begs John not to reveal her past. John goes ahead anyway and tells everyone that Harriet was raised by wolves, which would explain her pouncing on, and savagely devouring a roasted chicken being served at Tim's as the other guests looked on with shock and revulsion. Everyone is relieved to hear that it's nothing serious.

Daze Of Our Lives: Billy Bob confides in Alice that he's still in love with Darla who has just married Vince in the prison yard. Laureen gets Jim out of the house on the pretense that his sister Robin, who is in the hospital after being shot in a freak hunting accident, has spoken for the first time in months. Jim tells Laureen that he could never understand why Robin wore that Bullwinkle costume during hunting season. When he leaves, Adam comes out of the liquor cabinet where he has been hiding. Gary, upset that he has no siblings to bicker with, spends late nights in the lab trying to clone himself a twin. Zac is on the run from the police after a hit and run accident leaves Kendrick in critical condition and believing he is Confucius. Kendrick and Robin end up in the same hospital room and take bets on which one will go into a coma first. Sylvia, the wicked nurse with a mysterious past, bonks them both over the head with a bed pan, and it's a photo finish.

One Restless Life: There is a closed coffin at Dirk's funeral which leaves much speculation as to whether he is really dead. Sissy spots a man resembling Dirk working at a Seven-Eleven, and when she goes back he is pulling away in a convertible with a man Sissy believes to be Elvis. Collin thinks it was Uncle Joe who went over the cliff in that car, not Dirk. Ned has an affair with Linda, who is cheating on Dave, who is cheating on Barbara, who is in a coma. Jason who bears a remarkable resemblance to Larry, but is not related, assumes his identity while he is out of town on business, until Dexter, Jason's disturbed twin who has been under

Fleeting Thoughts

observation after taking part in a government experiment involving new hallucinogenic drugs, arrives, puts Jason in a coma and assumes Barbara's identity. Barbara (Dexter) discovers Dirk hiding in her clothes hamper, and they elope. Madge sees them leaving town in the back of a convertible driven by a man who bears an incredible likeness to Elvis.

Michael McGan

TERRIBLE TWOS... AND THREES... AND FOURS...

I called in to work one day because I was sick. It happened to be that one day of the week that explains why you're going to your stinking job at all. I called a friend I work with, asked him to grab my paycheck and bring it home with him. I would drive to his house later and pick it up. It was a good plan, a twenty minute ride through country roads, get the check, deposit the money, and go back home before I really started feeling lousy. A good plan, unless of course you had a *two year old* in the back seat! It was a stupid plan. It was madness.

The day was very hot and the humidity was very high. I was running a low grade fever so I felt like I was driving through Nairobi. My daughter was very tired, very cranky and very vocal. She was talking a-mile-a-minute, asking dozens of questions dozens of times. "Where's the policeman Dad?" This came as she was actively climbing out of her car seat.

"Where's the cows?" "Where's the horsies?" "Where we goin' Dad?" Then came the whining and crying. Then she dropped her book on the floor. "Dad, get my book. I dropped my book." "Dad!" "Dad!"

The sweat was poring out of me like a lawn sprinkler. I was getting woozy. I thought I saw Fidel Castro drive by in a Chevy Vega. I turned on the radio and to my relief, everyone was speaking

Fleeting Thoughts

English. I turned off the radio. I swerved to avoid a dead skunk. "What you doin' Dad?" If you've ever been a parent, you know that sometimes you don't volunteer information. Especially if doing so will require you to go into a lengthy and confusing explanation of everything in the universe, making up much of it as you go along because: (1) it will be more interesting to your child, and (2) you don't really have a clue anymore.

We eventually made it to my friend's house. He handed me my check and said I looked like crap. I thanked him and off we drove to the bank. Inside the bank I went to one of those counters where they want you to get prepared before you get to the actual teller window. Anyhow, I set my daughter down, tried to sign my check and make out a deposit slip. Seconds later from across the room, I heard "Dad! Look at the fish!" There was an aquarium. "Dad!" And finally, "Hey Mike!" I was glancing over my shoulder, trying to watch her and remember my account number all at the same time. Remembering my account number is hard enough when I'm alone and seemingly focused.

I picked her up and asked myself why I was doing this. Through the fog came the answer - if I didn't deposit this money today, we would be bouncing checks. I was asking myself if that was such a bad thing, compared to this, as I got in line. It was a long line. I knew she'd be whining before we got to the window so I gave her the empty envelope and said "Here's your check. Give it to the girl at the window."

Michael McGan

She opened the envelope wide and set it on my head. "Burger King, Dad. OK?" The ladies in the line were smiling at her while giving me this look that said, "Isn't she adorable?" Three hours with her and they'd all be spending their paychecks on massages, stiff drinks - maybe even therapy. I thought about Burger King. It sounded like a good idea. I should eat something.

I was standing at the counter trying to order when she pulled loose from my hand and ran to the far corner of the restaurant. A family of four were enjoying their meal when suddenly they became a family of five. I could see the look of confusion and horror on the woman's face as she tried to account for this new child. My daughter turned and pointed at me, indicating to the woman who was responsible for this intrusion. Then she smiled and began to wave at me.

I turned around and finished ordering, hoping that she wouldn't help herself to their food. I came to the conclusion that if you are ever with a small child, you should never, never choose to go inside any place that offers a drive-up window. I was thinking that drive-up windows had to be invented by someone with children, for the express purpose of avoiding situations like this. This person should have received the Nobel Prize. Or at least a free "value meal". On the way home the questions resumed. I felt like my frazzled brain held about as much information as Jell-O. And it was just barely jiggling.

Fleeting Thoughts

We arrived at home and like some kind of zombie. I got her washed up and ready for bed. She didn't protest; as I left her room I could hear her talking to herself. I was now talking to myself as well. I took some Tylenol and sat down on the sofa. I felt myself slipping slowly from the frenzied, feverish world into that much more beautiful world of peaceful sleep. I took a deep breath and thought that those ladies were right, she really is adorable. *Terribly* adorable. I thought of her turning three in a couple of months and wondered if the world was ready for another year. On this particular night, I wasn't ready for another minute. zzzzzzz.

I remember this day like it was yesterday, even though eleven years have past. Where did that time go? Time is a funny thing.

Michael McGan

NICE PLACE, DOLL FACE

Let's talk about the current Barbie and Ken for a moment here. You might be saying "Why is he talking about them again?" Well if you have young girls in your house you know that you can't escape Barbie and Ken. Besides, there's too much humorous material here to pass up. So let's get started.

Despite their good looks, neither one of them or any of their spinoffs have a job to speak of, yet they have everything that you and I can only dream of. Only on a much smaller scale. Who wouldn't want a pink Corvette convertible? Well, neither would I, but that's what paint is for. They have a "dream house", a pool, rooms full of clothing, all the food they can eat, jet-skis, four-wheelers, an RV, a condo in St. Martin, a booming E-business, and hidden bank accounts in the Caymans. How did they get all this? Plastic!

CREDIT CARD APPLICATION EXAMINER: What is your occupation?

BARBIE: I'm a doll.

CREDIT CARD APPLICATION EXAMINER: And what does that entail?

BARBIE: I wear lots of outfits, get my hair brushed, sit around...

CREDIT CARD APPLICATION EXAMINER: This card is at 34% interest.

BARBIE: Whatever.

Fleeting Thoughts

CREDIT CARD APPLICATION EXAMINER: Can you make the payments?

BARBIE: No way.

CREDIT CARD APPLICATION EXAMINER: You're approved.

They have countless tiny credit cards that, like many of their countless tiny accessories, are often lost moments after the package is open. Earrings, watches, bracelets, rings etc…. that are so small even Barbie and Ken can't find them. Mr. Hoover does though. You can always tell by that familiar sound, you have just sucked up part of their extensive jewelry collection. It feels good in a way, doesn't it?

They've got way too much, more than they'll ever need. Your child won't miss it, they have been warned several times not to leave this stuff strewn all over the house. Do they listen? Nooooo. Late at night, on your way to the bathroom if you step on one of Barbie's high heels you'll know what I'm talking about. Not as bad as a Leggo, but it will get your attention. So up and away they go. Barbie and Ken will just smile and claim it on their home owner's insurance, so it's all for the best.

When our girls, played with their Barbies, would spend hours digging through boxes of "Barbie Stuff" that are usually arranged in such a way that if you could imagine taking all five or six of your junk drawers, and dumping them into one container, shaking it violently for thirty seconds or so, it would have the same sense of organization.

Eventually they would set up the house, arrange the furniture, dress the dolls, and by then it would be time for the kids to go to bed. Now they would have to quickly change the dolls into pajamas and get *them* ready for bed. This will take another thirty minutes. The thing about playing with Barbie dolls, from my observation, is that it breaks down to 95% preparation, and 5% action. Action would be described as you physically moving the dolls around and doing their voices. Young girls creating conversation between these "adult" dolls is worth turning the TV down for.

Ken and all his male counterparts are just pretty boys that Barbie and her female friends toy with, (no pun intended) and then dispose of. I remember one time when I assumed the role of manipulating Ken he was looking a bit rough because his head had been pulled off at some point and was lost for a while. It later turned up under the sofa, scratched and chewed up pretty badly. It seems the cat might have had something to do with this. But the heads pop right back on, and you're back in business. Exchanging the heads of Barbie and Ken, (all in the interest of science of course) is guaranteed to get big laughs from your kids.

Anyway, I reunited Ken's newly found head with his body and even though he looked like something from a horror movie, he was brimming with

Fleeting Thoughts

confidence, although he was displaying a terribly disfigured smile. I put him in the Corvette and pulled up to the house making a noise like a car horn beeping. "Hey baby, wanna' go for a ride?" Barbie giggled and said, "OK." There was a brief Kung Fu fight between the two, then they settled down and got in the car.

Ken drove like a psycho and of course they had a terrible accident. There wasn't a scratch on the Corvette and Barbie escaped injury. Ken was not so lucky. He had been thrown an incredible *two* feet from the car, and was banged up pretty bad, as indicated by his arms and legs being forced into impossible positions, not to mention the fact that his head was on backwards. My man Ken had to be hospitalized.

He was taken to the residence of Barbie, which is of course the only building in town, and now served as "Our Lady of Barbie Memorial Medical Center General Patton Hospital". Here, he was given the best of medical care along with all kinds of sympathy and loving attention from an attractive woman, who was not a doctor, a licensed nurse, or a CNA. Who cares? Certainly not Ken! See? I know how to play this game.

Michael McGan

LITTER BY LITTER

Do you ever wonder if dogs remember their families? Let's suppose that they try. Fathers? They have no recollection of this guy. He's long gone by the time of delivery, chasing UPS trucks down that old lonesome road. Mothers? They probably do remember, and they should after sucking them dry for eight weeks or so. Brothers and sisters? I'm sure they do, but because of such poor phone skills and penmanship, they rarely communicate. One of my dog's sisters is with Howard Stern. She probably has some good stories to tell.

Here's what it might sound like if a group of canine siblings had a reunion:

Litter Mate #1: "Hey, you knew I was going to that farm in Oswego, you couldn't look me up? C'mere and let me sniff your butt!"

Litter Mate #2: "Listen, I'm sorry. I ended up two hundred miles away in the suburbs somewhere with this wild pack of humans. There's seven kids! You wouldn't believe the abuse I've endured."

Litter Mate # 3: "Stop your whining, both of you. You're doing OK, right?" (The sound of dogs mumbling to the affirmative) "You're both lookin' good. really. As for me, I'm with this sweet elderly lady who feeds me steak every night." (One and Two exchange glances, and then begin to sniff Three's butt.)

Fleeting Thoughts

Litter Mate # 4: "Every night? I'm so jealous. What a life, you mangy cur!"

(The sound of dogs enjoying a hearty laugh.)

They reminisce about their brief time together, back in the old days - their favorite blanket, their favorite bush etc. They share tricks they have learned, their trips to the vet, cat chasing experiences, and how many bones they have put away for retirement. They scratch and lick long into the night. It's a beautiful thing.

Michael McGan

A COLD BREW AND A HOT BIRD

Every year at Thanksgiving we are reminded of the Pilgrims. The image of those wild Puritan clothes making us thankful for the never ending voyage of fashion. What we remember most about the Pilgrims was the famous dinner celebration. Their guests considered by the Pilgrims to be savagely chic were the Indians, as they were mistakenly called. They were on the A-list of the Pilgrims who just knew that this group would soon be invited to the functions of everybody who was anybody. Invitations were sent out for the event to be held on a tentative date. As it turned out everyone from both groups had the day off and could attend.

The Pilgrims had a very tough trip over here on the Mayflower. Without the ability to properly bathe, along with the close living spaces of the crew and passengers, we can only imagine that this ship smelled like anything *but* a Mayflower. After a while dinning with the captain wasn't such a big deal, and their cruise itinerary, at first exciting, soon became routine and tedious. This itinerary was filled with such things as shuffleboard, tae-bo and skeet shooting with blunderbusses. Nothing to make light about. It is written that the real reason they didn't continue on to find Virginia, where they had permission to settle, was that they were running low on victuals, especially beer! I'm almost positive that this is

Fleeting Thoughts

absolutely true because at one time I was working in a pub where I read this from a calender put out by the makers of an English beer. Anyway, it does make sense.

Captain of the Mayflower: "Arrrrhhh. Bringeth me a fresh mug while ye be about. What sayeth thee, mate?

First Mate: "Captain, there be no more to drink. The kegs are empty!"

Captain of the Mayflower: "Shiver me timbers! This does not bode well. We'll have to pull over somewhere. Arrrrhhh."

If this *is* true, then their landing at Chrysler/Plymouth Rock was basically just a beer run. With the lack of convenience stores back then it was quickly decided that they would have to settle in and brew their own. Half of the people who arrived did not make it through the brutal cold and starvation of the first winter. Adding to their misery was the fact that they had no suds to wash down their meager supply of salted cashews. Nevertheless, in the spring the Native Americans showed the survivors how to grow crops such as corn and squash.

The Pilgrims said things like, "Hey, that's great!" and "Yum! I can taste it now!", but pestered them for the necessary grains required in the making of beer and ales.

Michael McGan

They were very grateful to the Native Americans and invited them to a harvest celebration dinner. This eventually got under way when the Pilgrims were done parading around for no apparent reason. The Pilgrims repeatedly complimented the Native Americans on their jewelry, makeup and designer clothing, and even thanked them for all their help to which they would reply: "You're welcome Pilgrim", and then blow chickpeas through a straw at the startled foreigners.

An air of tension soon descended on the gathering because of this, so it was decided that things would be settled by drawing up two teams and throwing a deceased pig around in an early version of football. For all the women who do not understand why men sit around watching hours of football on this day, you can now see why it is an integral part of Thanksgiving.

Scenes depicting this feast show it to be outside on large picnic tables. Also in these scenes, spray cans of insect repellent on the tables, would to the highly trained eye of a historian, suggest that this dinner certainly took place not in November, but in warmer weather. Perhaps September. The official day for this holiday has been changed so many times over the centuries that every day of the year has at some point been declared Thanksgiving Day.

Soon other settlers came and "Cape Flounder" was born and later changed to "Cape Cod" by the then Governor Steven Smith who was just fond of cod.

Fleeting Thoughts

Smith ran a profitable business chartering whale watching expeditions. He later sold the business and went into the salt water taffy trade, only to lose everything, including the Governorship of the colony when he insisted the people were ready for cranberry flavored taffy. But by this time the settlers were sick of cranberries and Smith's gamble was a disaster. He became a broken man spending his days walking the beach and giggling at seagulls.

But his story doesn't end there. He later regained his senses and invented stuffing, which got him back in the game in a big way, although he had to resist the urge to mix the bread crumbs with taffy. We are all thankful for that. Only it is unclear as to what was stuffed in the early stages of Thanksgiving. Probably duck or goose, along with venison, clams, eels, bread, wild plums, wine, and lemon marange pie - these were the staples of the early holiday meals.

Records show that it wasn't until years later at a meeting of the colonists to designate the official main course of Thanksgiving dinner that the fickled finger of fate pointed to the answer. As the question was raised, a man sitting next to Samuel Hopkins, a worldly traveler who was hearing impaired, asked where he got such a nice mohair sweater. "Turkey" he loudly replied, and all heads began to nod with agreement. Turkey it was, and ex-Govenor Steven Smith was pleased to hear the news because he had run the gamut from clams to cattle trying to find the perfect candidate for his procedure.

Michael McGan

Once, while under great stress to find the ultimate receptacle, he attempted to stuff the blow hole of a whale that had washed ashore. He was suddenly blown out of the harbor when the great creature awakened. Smith survived claiming he was rescued by Mermaids after which he invited to the upcoming Thanksgiving dinner. This was the beginning of the alternating holiday dinner system rotating between the Native Americans, the Pilgrims and the Mermaids. This has all been insidiously omitted from todays history books. Smacks of a conspiracy if you ask me.

As Thanksgiving draws near, reflect on all of this. Maybe have an English beer instead of wine with dinner. After all, for the want of a beer it all came to pass. Or so I've read, Pilgrim.

Fleeting Thoughts

TALK TO ME

Do I know you? I mean, really know you? Probably not if conversation has anything to do with it. We waste most of our time talking and not listening, gaining information. Everybody wants to talk about themselves. If they do ask a question about you, it's usually just something like- "How's it going?" "How you doing?" "How are you?" "Good", "Good", "Pretty Good'. Now what have we learned about you? Nothing. Maybe it's for the best.

It's going good, as opposed to going bad, which would be rotten. They're doing good, whatever it is they're doing. And they are pretty good, not to be confused with pirates, who "arrrh" pretty good themselves. Good, good, pretty good. All of this is no good. We need to ask better questions in order to get better answers. Here are some ideas. Try some of these questions on someone.

"Have you ever appeared on America's Most Wanted?" "Are you OK? You're not having an out of body experience or anything right now are you?" "Do you believe in leprechauns?" "Have you ever worked for the KGB?" "Do you believe Elvis worked for the KGB?" These are the kind of light, opening lines that give us quick glimpses of the person we are conversing with. Of course, they're answers could all be lies, so what do we do? We have to take some things on faith, give people the benefit of the doubt, which will allow us to move on and get to know them better. More questions.

"Are you wearing underwear right now, or are you going commando?" "Have you ever had anything lanced?" "How do you feel about the free and open use of mayonnaise?" "If I told you I was starting a new religion where an image carved from pepperoni was going to be worshipped, would you turn all your possessions over to me?" "OK, would you give twenty dollars?" See, now we're getting somewhere. Now we're starting to really get to know the person and what makes them tick. That's a good question!

"What makes you tick?" "Is that you ticking I hear right now?" "You're not wired or anything are you?" "Would you if you could, prefer to tock?" "Ticking and tocking are so different, wouldn't you agree?" "I myself am a tocker. Does this make you uncomfortable? Because I can just tick for awhile if you'd rather." "If you could fly anywhere in the world, where would you go?" "Would it bother you having a beak and feathers when you got there?"

We are beginning to see the whole picture, the whole person, without asking all those boring questions like: "Where do you live?" "What do you do for a living?" What exactly is a "living"? You can live, and you can be living, but you can't make or have a living. It just does not make sense. It's a trick question that I never know how to answer.

So try some of these questions at your next dinner party. Or come up with some of your own. Just

Fleeting Thoughts

remember to think outside the box when preparing your questions. If a parcel service came and took the box away to be mailed while you were thinking outside of it, how would this impact your wholeness?

Michael McGan

THE CASE OF THE DISAPPEARING WAITER

In the soft light, two lovers gazed across the table at one another. Outside, lightning flashed as the rain began to patter against the windows of Chez Vinny Ling's. Sirens wailed. Cheesecake was passed. The waiter Rod refilled their coffees. Rod had joined the restaurant staff only a month ago. He kept to himself and was quiet, except for an occasional chuckle for no apparent reason, after which he would glance furtively around the room.

Rod's hand began to tremble as the strolling violinist played the theme from "Love Story". The handsome couple at the table also began to tremble, because they really hated that song. Coffee spilled as the waiter could not control his shaking. Suddenly the lights went out causing screams and expletives. The strolling violinist played on in the dark until he was struck with a dinner roll, and vowed never to take requests again, except from his pet monkey.

When the lights came on again, the waiter was gone. There, where he had been standing, was an ice sculpture resembling Cupid. On the head of his arrow was a napkin which had on it the scribbled message, "Off to Tutango. Please forward the tip."

A strange puzzle indeed. It was only after all the confusion died down, it was noticed that a small handbag which had been on the floor next to the

Fleeting Thoughts

woman was also now missing. Upon becoming aware of this, she let out a shriek and fainted. The other half of the couple, this being the man, jumped from his seat to catch her as she slid toward the floor, but not before finishing off the last bite of cheesecake she had left on her plate. (Hey, like she'd remember?) She hit the floor with a thud as he tried to cry out her name only to be cut off half way through by a loud belch. He excused himself and attended to his dinner companion.

"Darling, are you alright?"

"Yes I think so," she said weakly, "Help me up."

He helped her back into her seat. She took a deep breath and let out a long sigh. "I can't believe it!"

"What is it? Your Bag?"

"No my cheesecake you pig! Please take me home now. I think I have a boat to catch." And with these words they were on their way. One of them far away.

It was a beautiful day in the South Pacific. There it sat, as a jewel afloat on the sea, its lush green landscape rushing to meet the magnificent white sand that surrounded it. Janet could not help thinking that she was approaching paradise as her ship closed the distance to the island. She had been a woman on a mission since the incident in the restaurant. Her friend Dilbert had offered to come with her but she needed to do this alone. Besides, he was a swine of a man.

Michael McGan

The pristine beauty of the island captured her eyes, and once on shore, the natives captured the rest of her. This was just a ceremony performed by the hotel staff to greet new arrivals. They were a fun loving people on Tutango. Their appearance was a curious blend of primitive tribal wear and techno-fashion. They all wore grass skirts and T-shirts displaying the image of a eight slice toaster along with the web site www. eightslice toasters.com.

As Janet finished slapping her mock captors out walked the hotel manager. "Welcome to Tutango. I'm sorry if you did not find our greeting to be endearing. My name Is Mangapu Snickers. I am the Mayor and Chief of the island people and Manager of The Wandering Palms Hotel. We are happy to have you with us Ms. Staples."

"Look I'm sorry myself for that stuff back there. I guess I'm just a little stressed out. How did you know my name anyway?"

"It was easy", said Mr. Snickers, "As you are the only female guest coming ashore today. You made reservations, remember? Come, let's get your things and we'll see to having you checked in. Your room is ready. I'm sure you'll find it suitable."

Later that evening Janet sat in the hotel bar and sipped a tropical drink. She was biding her time.

"So, how does a man of Tutango get a name like Snickers?" she asked the bartender.

"Here, we are given one name," he explained, "But as the island became more commercial most people

Fleeting Thoughts

took on what you call a surname. One day as Mangapu walked down the beach and watched the sunset he came upon what we now know to be a candy bar wrapper. He felt it was a religious experience and vowed to take "Snickers" as his new surname."

"I see." responded Janet. "And what is your last name Natti?"

"Kahlua," he answered. "Like on the bottle."

She noticed him walk in. She turned her head as he sat down and ordered a Shirley Temple. The cherry lodged in his esophagus as she sprang from her stool and grabbed him by the throat. "Hello Rod. I believe you have something of mine."

"It's here, honest! I have it." he choked.

"Natti, call Mr. Snickers. We have a problem here." she said as she let go of the gasping waiter.

Mr. Snickers and the hotel security quickly arrived and the bag was retrieved from Rod's room. (It was all starting to fit together, like the pieces of some bizarre, twisted puzzle falling into place. Even so, it still did not make a lick of sense.)

"Ms. Staples, is this what you're looking for?" asked Mangapu.

"My bag!" cried Janet as she feverishly searched inside.

"The money and cards are there. I didn't take anything." offered Rod.

"I didn't care about the money, it was this, that I dreaded losing." said Janet holding up a simple nail file.

"It was given to me by a very special Swami on the day he began his quest to be in the Guinness Book of World Records for the longest fingernails in the world. He set a record at twenty eight inches, but later in a fit of nervous tension due to a rivals posting of twenty seven and a half and growing, he began chewing and spitting in a frenzy. Nineteen people were sent to the hospital for lacerations and other injuries resulting from the near riot as people tried to flee the nail spitting Swami."

"I'm sorry I had no idea." said Rod.

"Why did you take my bag?"

"I wanted you to follow me Janet, and you did. You see, I fell in love with you that night at Chez Viny Ling's. I think it was the way you smugly picked through your salad, tossing the olives over your shoulder. I knew you would figure out that I had your bag, and that you would come.

"Really Rod?" Janet said with excitement.

"I knew," Rod went on, "That I must win your heart, but to do that, I had to get you far away from the rat race."

"So you stole my bag and left a clue as to where you could be found. And the ice sculpture?" Just a creative touch." said Rod, swelling with pride.

"Oh Rod!" purred Janet, "This was all so playfully romantic."

Fleeting Thoughts

"I thought so, but again, I didn't know about the file deal there. Must be special, huh?"

"Yes. The Swami was an inspiration to me, encouraging me to go for broke, shoot for the moon, reach for the stars..."

"I understand." interrupted Rod.

"I'm so confused Rod. I guess sometimes life just steals your handbag, and you have to go for broke, shoot for the moon, reach for the stars...Rod, are you listening?" snapped Janet. "What does it all mean?"

Rod was gazing out the window at a coconut tree, chuckling. "I'm sorry. What were you saying?" he replied, glancing nervously around.

"What does it all mean?" Janet repeated.

"Squat." said Rod.

Janet assumed the squatting position. "OK, what now?" Rod joined her and they looked at things from a new perspective.

"Hold me Rod! I think we were meant to be together or something!" The manager and security left shaking their heads as the squatting couple embraced, and then tumbled over.

Janet and Rod were married on the beach the next day. Mangapu Snickers performed the ceremony, being a religious man and all. They honeymooned at The Wandering Palms Hotel on the island of Tutango. The one which floated like a jewel in the sea.

Michael McGan

TOSSED IN SPACE

Light-year: the distance light travels in one year - six trillion miles. Right? Lite-beer: the official beer for speedy space travel, won't fill you up and cause countless trips to the restroom while rocketing through space. Now you know the difference. And when you're going that fast you can't worry about recycling. So just go ahead and heave the empties out the disposal hatch. Let some stupid alien get the deposit. Oh, I'm sorry. That wasn't nice. We shouldn't litter. Even in space. But come on, relax folks. Like we'll be going on picnics out there or something. "OK kids, grab your space-suits, the shuttle's all packed. We're going to have a nice day on Pluto!"

I think we should blast all our trash out into space. The astronauts are doing it. There's already a lot of crap in space. Literally. (Do you think they bring all that doody back to Earth with them?) How about this? No more dumps, no more landfills. Wouldn't that be nice? Those soiled Huggies thousands of miles out in space. If they did get back to the Earth's atmosphere they would burn up on re-entry anyway, so what are you worrying about. With all that methane out there, talk about your shooting stars! It would be a bonanza for stargazers.

"Isn't it beautiful Pearl? I know that had to be one of little Billy's. He's so full of it, you know?"

Fleeting Thoughts

Yeah, I know. It would get kind of messy out there with all our trash floating around. That's where the "Star Wars" laser technology would sure come in handy., blasting anything large and threatening that looks like it might come out of orbit and head back for Earth. We could even try to take out some of the other guy's satellites and say, "Oops. We're really sorry about that. Won't happen again. Promise."

This has actually been tried by the National Aeronautics and Space Administration (AARP) but the whole idea raised "significant political problems". Problems-schmoblems, let's blast away. Even *more* fun for stargazers. They would really make out with all of this. Space would become exciting, instead of...well you know, impressive and awe inspiring, yet kind of...dull, and useless to most of us poor slobs who can't afford prospecting asteroids. Oh yeah, that's going to be the next gold rush.

There's a company called SpaceDev that's already planning to land a private spacecraft on an asteroid to collect scientific data and more importantly, stake a claim, hoping that their mining results in the discovery of gold! Space towns, complete with saloons would probably soon follow. "I struck it rich! A round of drinks for everybody! I got gold nuggets comin' out of my asteroid!"

But getting back to a less attractive subject such as our trash, and the disturbing, politically problematic, yet brilliant plan that I fully support. When you really think about it, it sounds kind of reasonable doesn't it?

I can hear you now, "Yeah, actually that don't sound like a bad idear. The town wont pick up that old fridge that's been sittin' out front, and I've got no way to get rid of it sinse I let my brother Cletus borry my pick-up, and he wrecked it up real good. So if they blast it out there in space, well...can't see it from my house." Unless of course you buy a telescope. C'mon, there's already "space junk" out there now. More than ten thousand objects large enough to be tracked from the ground. Old rockets, you name it. The government could even raise money to support this idea by setting up booths at state and county fairs. Two dollars a shot!

NASA could get a whole new image. Big trucks rolling down your street getting rid of all your junk. On the side of the truck, in big letters...NASA. Everyone would then believe that they were getting something out of the space program besides a cable channel were nothing goes on, except boring satellite shots, or the scene where ten or twelve people are sitting around motionless in front of screens and monitors trying desperately to convey the appearance of consciousness. You could put manikins in those chairs and play cards in the break room. Nobody would know. I might apply.

So I think with the increasing need for land-fills and dump sites, which are a blight upon our fair countryside and take up precious space that could be devoted to sprawling theme parks and shopping

Fleeting Thoughts

malls, that we need to look skyward for the answer to rubbish removal.

Yes indeed, space would be different. Picture this:

"Adventurer to Houston - small craft spotted dead ahead. Could be that new Russian shuttle, the XKE Nordavich Roadster. Over?"

"Houston here Adventurer. Negatory good buddy. It appears to be, from what we can make out, a ... *Westinghouse side-by-side.* Over."

"Affirmative Houston. That's a positive ID. Looks like a real old model judging from that nasty old shade of green. Tell the laser guys to hold their fire. We're going to pull that sucker in. Our cooler is down and we could use it to chill these beers. Over."

"Hey Buzz, jettison that dryer we rescued last week. We need some room for this fridge. Lucky thing that we have an automatic navigation system to fly us safely through this endless, desolate void called space while we quaff a few frosty cold brewskies, eh? Ha ha ha. What the...? Houston, we have a problem. I think we were just struck by a ... *Lazy-Boy recliner!* Over."

"Adventurer? I've been told that one of the laser guys had his eye on that. Could you grab it for him? He says he'll slip you a twenty when you get back. Over."

"Roger that, Houston. We'll cram it in here somewhere. Over and out."

Michael McGan

SOMEWHERE OVER THE RAINBOW BRIDGE

In Norse mythology, and in one of my favorite comic books was the mighty Thor. He lived in a place called Asgard which was very cold. He had this big ol' hammer that he'd swing around. He did a lot of the home improvement projects in Asgard, which was chuck full of gods. These gods apparently were not very handy. Being gods and all you'd think they would have picked some place with more of a tropical setting for their home. But as a mere mortal, who am I to question these things? Maybe they moved to warmer climates when they retired, live on their pensions, savings, and social security.

Remember the guy who was the watchman on the Rainbow Bridge? Heimdall was his name. He'd be out there through eternity, guarding the way to Asgard, checking people out. He was The security guard of the gods.

Every day Nancy, the goddess of concessions would take the ice cream wagon out to "Heimi" on the Rainbow Bridge. "Heimi" who would wink at her with appreciation.

"Heimdall darling, put down that fishing pole. You haven't caught anything in eons. Have some refreshment."

"I grow tired of the same old creamy flavors Nancy. Do you have anything in a sherbet?"

Fleeting Thoughts

"Give me a few days, I'll think of something."

Sure Heimdall probably would have preferred to be the god of lightning or something but he was thankful that he had work. The residents of Asgard could sleep well at night knowing Heimdall was on the job. That is if they did in fact sleep, with their plans for hijinks and all. It seems that the major purpose of the gods was to play tricks on ordinary mortals back on Earth.

In one story we hear about Randy, the god of novelties, and his prank on Olaf the sheep herdsman. One evening after a long day of herding, Olaf returned to his digs only to find the floor covered with doo doo.

"Why those dirty sheeeep!" he screamed, only to hear howls of godlike laughter.

"Gotcha! They're fakes." yelled Randy, "Boy I'm good!" With his mission complete, Randy caught the 7:50 bus back to Asgard and began to skip back over the bridge, which was strictly for pedestrians and did not allow vehicles to pass over. Randy returned to the frosty land to plan another day of trickery.

"Whatcha got there Heimdall?"

"A new and colorful sherbet, Randy. How's the trickster business?"

"Oh those mortals! I could do this forever! Come to think of it, I have to! It's my job! Ha ha ha. Say, that is a very colorful treat you've got there. Could I try one?"

Michael McGan

"Sure can," said Heimdall, pulling a sherbet from one of several boxes. 'It was very warm out here earlier today for some reason. I think it was all the comet activity. One came so close that my back hair burst into flames." Randy chuckled at this. "Nancy tried to keep me refreshed, but some of her sherbets melted all over the bridge. Now it's freezing over again. Better watch your step Randy."

As Randy walked off laughing heartily, he slipped on a brilliant patch of frozen sherbet. "What the..." He nearly fell, but caught himself in time. "Ha ha ha. You almost got me Heimdall." Heimdall rolled his eyes and went back to licking his "Rainbow Sherbet", and salting the bridge.

And so it went, in the land of myth.

Fleeting Thoughts

IF YOU ONLY KNEW

I had no idea that there are so many psychics out there. Apparently they have rooms full of them waiting by the phones for you to call. I think maybe someone's faking, at least one or two of them. Do you want to know what's ahead for you? Is romance in your future? Will you get that promotion? Well, I guess you'll have to call them, because I couldn't tell you. Here's how it might go.

Psychic: "Hi! Welcome to Sykik Psy-line. What can I do for you?"

Caller: "Hi. I have a question about my boy friend. I don't trust him. I keep finding match books and napkins with phone numbers of different women on them. Is he running around on me? Are we headed for trouble?"

Psychic: "I see that your boy friend can not be trusted, and that you have had your doubts about him. You are a patient woman. You want to avoid trouble, yet, you need answers."

Caller: "Wow! That's amazing! How did you know that?"

Psychic: "Your boyfriend's name is...Donald?"

Caller: "No, it's Jerome. Shouldn't you know that?"

Psychic: "Jerome, Donald, whatever. He is indeed running around on you, and I see you confronting him with this."

Michael McGan

Caller: "Is Sheila that blonde from his office? I hope not. She's really twisted."

Psychic: "I can't really tell... Could be!"

Caller: "I knew it. Say, do you see us working this out? Because I think we can. I mean... I really would like to."

Psychic: "I see you trying to work this out, and he will soon give you something."

Caller: "Oh, really? That sounds exciting! Is it a ring? No, don't tell me. I want to be surprised. This has been great! You've really helped me here."

Psychic: "Well, we do what we can. Thank you for calling Sykik Psy-line.

Here is another example of a possible conversation:

Caller: "Hello? Is this the Psy-Line?

Pizza Parlor: "Toni's Pizzeria. How can I help you?"

Caller: "I'm sorry, you said your name was Toni P. Zarria? I have a date coming over tonight Toni, and I don't know what to make for dinner. I don't even know what she likes. What should I do?"

Pizza Parlor: "Well, I'm thinkin' she likes pizza. Pizza from this place called Toni's. Yeah, you get her some Toni's pizza, and your gonna be golden. Could I take that order for you?""

Caller: "Thank you so much!"

Alright, wrong conversation.

Fleeting Thoughts

Caller: "Howdy! This here is Tex. I need to know about my brother Lester. Is he gonna be OK?"

Psychic: "Well Tex, I think that despite being kicked in the head by a horse, Lester will fully recover and eventually take the raccoon off his head and come out of the Alamo."

Caller: "What in the hell are you talkin' bout? He wasn't kicked in the head by no horse. He fell from one of my oil rigs!"

Psychic: "Why yes... Tex. This is true, but... He's going to be kicked in the head by a horse! Yes, that's it! He will be bending down to pick up your ... fourteen carrot, diamond studded, money clip that's straining to hold a thick wad of bills, and... he will be kicked. But he's going to be OK."

Caller: "A fourteen carrot, diamond studded money clip, holdin' a big wad did you say?"

Psychic: "Yes Tex. There is more money in your future. And as far as Lester... He'll be OK."

Caller: "Well thank heavens. And thank you and the Psy-Line for makin' my day."

Psychic: "Ya'll come back now, hear?"

Michael McGan

A THREE HOUR CRUISE

I love the ocean. That is, when the water is warm and calm and there's a sturdy boat under me. My wife and I went on a sun set cruise off of Cape Cod. It was a beautiful evening and had all the potential for a classic sun set. The schooner bobbed in the waves and the sea breeze was refreshing. The captain called out points of interest as we headed further out. He had neither a wooden leg nor a hook. I don't recall him having a beard of any color or a parrot, but he seemed very capable of sailing none the less. There was one mate or hand, or whatever they're called, aboard a sea faring vessel.

We had barely finished our drink when the clouds began to roll in. At first it seemed as though it might just cloud up a bit as we continued out. Maybe mess up our sun set. We were wrong. It was getting very dark very quickly and the concern on the captain's face became evident. He would soon have to make the decision to continue on or turn and run for home. We were over an hour out at this point, and missing the sunset was now the least of our worries.

We were informed that storms that come in so quickly and look so menacing are not common there. Now don't get me wrong, this wasn't "The Storm Of The Century", but it was a good one. Trust me. We felt special. When the first flash of lightning lit up the now black sky, we were feeling really special. This

Fleeting Thoughts

was not going to be your run of the mill sunset cruise that everyone else gets. No sir, we were going to fight for our bloody lives! Special. It was time to make a run for home.

Being the only male on board other than the captain he must have just *assumed* I'd be willing to risk life, limb and my beer on deck while the women and children went below. Well not all of them. The first mate, who I think was the captain's significant other, was running around frantically. My courageous, lovely and talented wife also was put to work.

The captain ordered us to get the sails down quickly. When this was done he frantically yelled at me to, "Swing the boom into the boom-crotch!" Now under different circumstances this might have been sort of funny in a sophomoric way, and I would have shot back something incredibly witty like, "Huh?" But things being what they were, I looked around and found the first thing that looked like it might be construed as a big ol' crotch. I swung the thing I hoped was the "boom" into it with everything I had. The boom is the horizontal pole thingy that swings around wildly in all the movies and knocks people overboard, where they are quickly devoured by sharks the size of Bermuda.

Finally the boom was secure and we were now moving under the power of what at this time was to me man's greatest invention, the engine. We were heading back in and as the schooner fought through the rough sea, driving rain, stabs of lightning. The captain told us all that there would be no free drinks, hats or t-shirts, despite my subtle hints, but we could all come back tomorrow for a make-up cruise. Big deal. Most of us could use a little make-up right about now to put some color back in our ashen faces.

We didn't come back because we had to drive home the next day. Besides, we had just had too much fun that evening and knew that we couldn't top such an exhilarating experience, even if we did wear make-up. Nevertheless, we will never forget our "sunset cruise".

I wonder what a moonlight cruise would be like?

Fleeting Thoughts

WORD UP

As a parent, you know the reason that you have children is because they bring you joy. Talking to them can be a wonderful and enlightening experience. Sometimes. Perhaps this thought has entered your mind on a particular occasion. For example when one of them is trying to blast their music louder than the other. Yet somehow, despite the fact that you honestly believe that your eardrums have just exploded like stomped on milk cartons, you can still hear them yelling at each other, doors slamming, bodies thumping, screaming, crying, and so on. Here, you must pull yourself together and take action. As a sane and rational parent, you know what must be done. You must run away. Run like the wind! Just kidding. You must try to bring peace and stability back to your little world through effective dialogue with your children.

YOU: Hey, guys! Please stop it.
FIRST CHILD: I hate Amber!
YOU: That's not true, you're just upset right now.
FIRST CHILD: Yes it is true! I hate her, I hate her, I hate her!
YOU: No you do not. You're both being silly. Now what is this all about?
SECOND CHILD: She took my Dr. Dre CD without asking me.

Michael McGan

> FIRST CHILD: She punched me!
> SECOND CHILD: Because she pushed me!
> YOU: Alright. Let's all be nice. Amber, give the Dr. Drake CD back to Ashley. Ashley, you apologize for punching Amber, right now or you'll both be getting a time-out.
> FIRST CHILD: Here's your stupid CD back, you big dork!
> SECOND CHILD: You're the dork, you butthead!

Accusations, shoving and fighting flare up once again despite your use of what you believed to be effective dialogue. The thought of bribery may cross your mind but then you are just setting yourself up for an ever increasing monetary demand for compliance. You picture big, stretch limo's picking them up to go to the dance. Meanwhile, you're in the kitchen throwing ziti's into a cup with your last herbal tea bag and calling it soup, checking out the canned dog food because those beef chunks in gravy always did look pretty good. This disturbing scenario brings you back to your senses. At this point, you will see that talking to them is still the best solution, even if you have to break through their comfort zone a bit. You just may come to the conclusion that it's time for some old fashion, and *really* effective dialogue to get their attention.

> YOU: (bad word). I've had enough of this (bad word)! Knock it off, right now! Both of you turn down that (string of bad words) excuse for music! And if I

Fleeting Thoughts

hear one more sound from either one of you, You're gonna' be sorry! Aaaarrrgghhhhh!!! **(bad word)**!

FIRST CHILD: Dad sounds like a *rapper!*
SECOND CHILD: Yeah. Maybe we should really listen to what he says!
FIRST CHILD: We could record him and put it to music! Make a CD!
SECOND CHILD: Yeah! That would be so *cool* ! "Snoop Doggy Dad"!
FIRST CHILD: I'm sorry.
SECOND CHILD: Me too. C'mon, I'll do your hair.

Suddenly, by talking to your children you have affected their actions in a positive way. You have brought them together and given them purpose, a plan for the future. It's important to have a plan.

Michael McGan

THE DOGS OF WAR AND PEACE

Modern technology has sure made things easier. We can go places that we never could before. So can dogs. As I approached the entrance to the library one fine day the doors slid open triggered by some kind of sensor. Inside there was a dog walking briskly around, tail wagging. He was inside, and he thought it was great!

From behind the desk I heard one librarian say to another, "He's in here all the time. Him and another dog." (not very good grammar for a librarian is it?) "They come up the ramp, the doors open, then they just come in."

They don't know any better. There's no sign which says that dogs are not allowed, at least I don't recall seeing one. And even if there was, they can't read. Hah!

When I was leaving a man came to the desk and said, "Alright, where is he?" He must have been the library bouncer. The librarian said, "He's downstairs in the children's section."

Of course! Where else would he be? None of that high-brow stuff for him, he's down there where the books have pictures. Dogs and children are a lot alike. They have short attention spans, poor toilet skills, and are always moving. Most dogs are also very social and playful, just like most children. There are exceptions in both groups.

Fleeting Thoughts

I could see him down there, tail wagging, kids petting him and handing him copies of "Clifford The Big Red Dog". He's probably having a good time, and then the "heat" busting in and chasing him around.

"Hey Spike! Where are you? We gotta' get out of here. Make a break for it and I'll meet you back at the hideout!" Canine Adventure Stories: 344.C.

Michael McGan

PERHAPS A DIP - AT THE LAKE

High above the ground, floating effortlessly on the strong wind, a red hawk stretched his wings and sat there like a corked bottle in the middle of a still pond. He didn't move, he just seemed to be staring out over the lake at the horizon as the wind held him in place.

I wondered what message was in this corked bottle. I thought of how the Native Americans might have said this was a sign. I thought of the Native Americans because the building I was in, is said to be on the site of what was once, among other things, an "Indian settlement", overlooking Saratoga Lake.

So was there a message here with this hawk? Some messages are easily misread. Sometimes, despite our eager interpretations, there really is no message, it's just a random event. "The ending to Tab's story leaves us to wonder. Does anyone think they know what he was trying to tell us?" (You're kidding right?) "I think he was saying that although Pete fell from the Empire State Building, this was a beautiful thing in that.... I don't know. I had something there... but I'm losing it." See what I mean?

But as my dust mop glided across those hardwood floors like a hawk on the wind, I got to thinking about one man who's misunderstood message became his claim to fame. This man as it turns out, was half Stockbridge Indian. He also worked right on this very

Fleeting Thoughts

same piece of property. You might say this guy had a chip on his shoulder. His name was George Crum.

In 1853, a man named Cary Moon opened the now famous Moon's Lake House right on this spot. In the kitchen there were two chefs, a woman known as "Aunt Kate" and George Crum. Mr. Crum had been a guide in the Adirondack Mountains until becoming trained in the culinary arts by a Frenchman called "Frenchie", someone he had met in his travels. Sometime after this, he claimed that he could take anything edible and turn it into a meal fit for a king.

At Moon's Lake House, he delighted customers with meals equal to his ego. Occasionally someone would make the mistake of asking that something be taken back to the kitchen. This so infuriated the volatile Mr. Crum, that he would send back to the table something totally disgusting. He would peer out from the kitchen to watch the customer's reaction. Many would just get up and leave. He got a kick out of this.

One day a man complained that his French fried potatoes were not made to his satisfaction. He wanted them thinner and had them sent back to the kitchen. Mr. Crum was furious. He sliced some potatoes wafer thin, wrapped them in a napkin and put them in ice water for a while. He then took them and threw them in a kettle of boiling grease. When they were done, he salted them and had them sent out to the table as he watched and waited for the customer's reaction.

Much to his surprise the customer loved them and passed them around to others who soon requested them. The potato chip was born, created by a real "wise" guy. The next day, Saratoga Chips were on all the tables. The rest is history.

What is not so well known, is that this drove some of his competitors to great lengths trying to come up with something equally as impressive. Through my own extensive research I have learned of a man named "Floppy Joe" Kloeg, who worked for a restaurant in town, and feverishly tried to perfect a distinctive sandwich using ground duck, minced onions, and chili sauce. He was so close. After witnessing several customers exhibit violent, yet colorful displays of projectile vomiting, he lapsed into the state of depression, and then left for some other state. Texas, I think.

Jake Borstrom opened a small restaurant on the other side of the lake, called "Jake's Small Restaurant On The Other Side Of The Lake". Although not a chef himself, he had his cooks work on what he thought would be his masterpiece: baked fish cubes dipped in chocolate. But chocolate covered fish cubes never caught on as Borstrom had dreamed they would. He closed his place a defeated man, saying that he was going to seek some badly needed rest. Later was often seen gulping mineral water at the many springs in town.

Others desperately tried to cash in on the "chip" thing, and focused their efforts in that area alone.

Fleeting Thoughts

Probably the most notable, was "Big Dan" Gleason, a well known but delusional chef working at his brother Gerry's place called, "Brother Gerry's Place". "Big Dan" wanted to make the ultimate chip. He was fond of saying, "Why do you think they call me 'Big Dan'?" To this day no one knows, but for his chip, he chose thickly sliced buffalo meat, soaked for days in tubs of cold beer, then quick fried in very large vats of hot grease.

Michael, another sibling working in the kitchen, once scoffed at Dan's idea only to be struck over the head with a large skillet. Soon after this incident he seemed distant, apathetic, and talked of joining the ballet. There was now the heated air of tension in the kitchen, despite Gerry's installation of exhaust fans.

"Big Dan's Big Buffalo Chips" were doomed from the start. Almost as large as the tables and as thick as a phone book, they were just too big. But he bitterly refused to compromise on their size, again asking, "Why do you think they call me 'Big Dan'?" With his frightened customers quickly disappearing, Gerry moved his business to Boston in the middle of the night, as Dan slept off one of his big beer soaked buffalo chips.

George Crum and his potato chip could not be outdone. Moon's Lake House became a landmark. It later went through many transitions but there is still a restaurant on that site. It's now called Cohan's. And there I am, mopping the floors of history, observing nature, and waiting for my chip to come in.

Michael McGan

OVER THE RIVER AND TROUGH THE BOOTHS

The Bridge To The Twenty First Century is all we heard about as we came up on the big day. "We're building the bridge." "We're getting on the bridge." "We're moving across the bridge." They were really pushing this whole bridge thing on us. After a while, hearing all of this may have driven some people to consider "taking the bridge", and slowly drifting down that lazy river to the sea.

What the heck was the rush to get into the next millennium? Did they give away prizes or something to the first people through the door? Expectations and preparations were huge. Excitement and anxiety rose to a fever pitch. When it was the seventies, the eighties, did we have all that pressure? No we didn't.

And why do we need a bridge all of a sudden? Is there a bridge leading back to the nineteenth century? Lots of people would like to get on that one. Wherever we're going, into the twenty-first century and beyond, we'll get there eventually. Or, there's always the chance we could wake up some morning and our world will be one big, stinky, smoldering piece of toast. Who knows?

It felt like this to me: like we were kids, riding in the back of the station wagon on the way to the fair. We've just crossed the bridge, and up front, Dad is saying to Mom, " I'm ready to bust myself Blanche!"

Fleeting Thoughts

"It's all that bran. You should have gone before we left!"

"There's no goin' back! I've got it pinned! You kids hold on now. If I hit that little incline at the gate just right, we can sail over the sand sculpture, bounce on through the 4-H building, and be right at the bathrooms before anybody else gets in there and stinks them up!"

"Dad, That's sick! Can't you hold it? Slow down! We'll get there eventually."

"Jack we're going to run somebody over! Blow the horn!"

"We're comin' up on the entrance!"

"Look Mom, the gate's not even open yet!"

"Oh my God Jack, we're early!!!"

So before we got into that car to head across the bridge to the big fair, we needed to take time to cleanse ourselves of any deep seated anxiety about the future. After all, maybe there's a new attraction or two, but it's always pretty much the same fair it was last year isn't it? Are we there yet? Well, yes we are as a matter of fact! Is life magically different now? Well, no it's not, but all that hype and bridge crossing stuff sure was exciting wasn't it?

"Dad when your pants are dry and you can come out of there, can we get some cotton candy?"

Michael McGan

NOTHING TO SNEEZE AT

Humanity's leading illness is the common cold. If you have a cold as I do right now, you have come into contact with one of two hundred viruses. Your body is like a big hotel. A virus checks in and before you know it, all your rooms are full of their reproduced twins. Once your body tires of catering to these pesky ingrates, they are booted out and not allowed to return for three to ten years! This is called immunity. Now you just have to worry about the other one hundred and ninety nine different cold viruses checking in. At the desk we ask, "Have you stayed with us within the last ten years? Oh I'm sorry...Get the hell out of here!"

Where does a cold virus go when it leaves you? Well you've probably infected someone else you schmuck, which keeps the whole thing going. Somebody, somewhere is keeping each virus alive. But you must not worry about all this because then you will be under stress—which doubles your chances of catching a cold.

Have ever told somebody, "Cover your mouth when you sneeze."? Well there's good reason to do this because when we sneeze we send millions of virus particles into the air. If a person has covered their mouth as requested, they have prevented this. However, they now have millions of virus particles on their hand, which they will then use to touch

Fleeting Thoughts

everything in the room. They will now go out of their way to touch things. Anything. Thank you so much.

You would have to isolate yourself from the rest of humanity in order to avoid these viruses. What's the big deal? So we get colds and they stay with us, irritate the staff and generally trash the place for a week or two. They remind us that feeling good shouldn't be taken for granted.

You'll have to excuse me now, as I have to go put these mints on the pillows.

Michael McGan

GIVE IT TO ME BABY

Sex, lies, and video tapes. OK, so there's no sex, but when you go down to Video Atlantis and you're looking for a particular tape, what do you do when you look at that empty shelf? Say you're desperate for the latest action movie, or that hit comedy that just came out on video. You walk in all jazzed up, ready to pick up your entertainment for the night. But it's not meant to be.. "I'm sorry, all our copies are out for the night."

"No. No! It has to be tonight!" you're thinking. You have to move quickly to the next name in your little black book of video membership. Now you're at the point where you have to be tactful. Sure, this is your favorite store but you don't want the owner to know you're seeing someone else. "Ahh, you know, I think I'll just watch what's on TV tonight and try again tomorrow." Sure. They know you're lying. They know where you're going. You're going down the street to Video Wonderland. You feel cheap and sleazy but you've got to have it.

You speed down the street, picturing someone else's grubby hands reaching out to touch your movie, to take it home with them. You run in expecting the worse, but there it is waiting for you. The last copy. How could you have doubted?

Brimming with relief and nervous anticipation, you drive home with your movie, reaching over to

Fleeting Thoughts

cover it with your hand as you pass Video Atlantis. They're sitting there in the window, "There he goes. I'll bet he got what he wanted elsewhere." "Yeah, they're all the same. Oh well, he'll be back. He always comes back."

Later, as you're sitting down in front of the fire with your movie and some wine, you get a call. "Hey Greg, This is Fred over at Video Atlantis. I have a copy of that movie you wanted here. Somebody brought it right back. You still want it?"

They know what you're up to. They're making you sweat. Laying on the guilt "Ahh, you know Fred, I have a nasty headache now, so... I think I'll pass tonight. Maybe some other time."

"Sure. I understand."

Oh what a tangled web we weave.

Michael McGan

THE KING AND THE BIG FACE
(A Fairy Tale)

Once upon a time there was a mighty king who was very unhappy. Although he was the ruler of the kingdom and was married to the queen, who was a real babe, he felt that there was something missing in his life. So one day, he set off on a journey to find whatever it was that was missing.

Over great mountains and through beautiful valleys he pressed on until nightfall. He fell soundly asleep under the stars, and suddenly in a dream, the king was face to face with a big face. He did not recognize the frightful face, yet it seemed so familiar to him. The king was terrified, but not wanting to lose face, he knew he must face the face.

"What is it that you search for, wandering king?"

"Why, I am not certain, oh, Big Face. In truth, I do not know what it is I search for" said the king, "But surely something is missing in my life."

"You do not recognize me do you?" said the big scary face, "I am the face of your collective subjects."

"Sheesh, I thought I had better looking subjects." mumbled the king.

"What you search for is my acceptance, that and your favorite slippers which one of your servants hid behind a wine barrel in the Royal Banquet Hall. The acceptance you must find for yourself. When you

Fleeting Thoughts

awaken, go back to the castle and address your subjects. You will know what to say. And on your way back, don't look up."

With this, the big face disappeared. The king woke up and began to walk back to his castle. On his way he encountered a magic bird who flew by and soiled his robes with bird crap. But it was magic bird crap. He began to curse the bird, but suddenly he started laughing. The king had not felt this good in a long time. He laughed and giggled all the way back to the castle, where he called all his subjects together.

"Greetings my fellow countrymen. I've called you all here to tell you that I have had an experience on my journey that has enlightened me. I realize that I have been soiling on you for quite some time now. This must end. Further more, we need to have less drudgery, and more yuks!

I also had a dream in which a big face told me to address you. And so, I'll start with you there. You'll be at number 9 Moat Lane, and you... Just kidding! Lighten up people! I'm reducing your taxes, and having you all over for dinner tonight. A feast!"

The king's subjects were delighted and embraced him. Not literally of course, especially with that bird crap on his robes. "I decree that all dry cleaners that have been detained in the dungeons will be released, by Royal Proclamation! Here, take these robes! And fetch my slippers in the Royal Banquet Hall!"

Michael McGan

And so, the king found what he was looking for and together with his subjects, lived happily ever after—more or less.

Fleeting Thoughts

NOPLACIA LIKE HOME

This may need a little bit of an introduction, so here we go. Two monsters, Moreiga and Gilethra are sitting by the sea shore talking when they are joined by a third monster. (By monster, I'm talking about those four hundred foot tall, funky dinosaur type monsters like in those Japanese movies from the 50s and 60s.) During their conversation the two original monsters find that Hythlodan, their new friend, is a well traveled monster.

In the lengthy discussions which follow, Hythlodan tells how in most places it's every monster for himself, but on a certain remote and distant island things are quite different. They take a break in the talks long enough to devour some fishing boats, their crew and cargo, and then Hythlodan gives a detailed account of his time living on ...Montopia.

"After being awakened by nuclear testing, I began to swim until I came upon a wonderful island. It was a very large island which made it suitable for monsters of all shapes and sizes. There was even an expansive, open area where flying monsters could land and take off, not that they would voluntarily leave this place, but sometimes they had to leave for matters of business.

The island was originally conquered and named by a monster called Montopus who ruled as prince until he fell into an erupting volcano and presumed to be killed. He later turned up on the other side of the world menacing some country villages en route to a larger city with power lines, heavy traffic and all. The prince, together with the elected council of monsters is responsible for settling all issues concerning the population.

Each monster must work at something based on their skills and preference. Some may be on the hunter/gatherer committee, providing food which is either flame broiled by those with fiery breath, or internally cooked in seconds by those with radioactive breath. Others may be on the cave development committee tending to uniform housing for all monsters. Others still may be on the building committee, constructing mock human cities for practice in the art of destruction and mayhem. They do this not out of enjoyment, but necessity, as part of their make up. Hey, there monsters!

So they work at these types of things during a short workday of only six hours, giving much free time for the finer things in life such as monster wrestling which is enormously popular. Imagine, huge creatures throwing each other around, pretending to hurt each other, with no apparent rules of combat.

There is a small group of monsters who are exempt from physical labor because of their higher intelligence. They devote their time to things such as the study of astrology because they have to watch for hostile monsters from space. Ones like Gidran, the

Fleeting Thoughts

nine headed, fire breathing monster, who will come and disrupt their near perfect society. They also keep track of the number of inhabitants on the island.. If the population of monsters on the island exceeds the limit set by the council, volunteers are sent off to terrorize the country of their choice.

And then there are the island philosophers whose chief job is determined the source of true happiness. Most agree that stomping, burning, and generally crashing through human cities in foreign countries is highest on the list. This is a pleasure. Any normal bodily function is also considered a pleasure: eating, drinking, roaring, blowing atomic smoke rings and enjoying good health, as opposed to being reduced to dust particles, being incinerated, sent to mars, you know, those kind of things.

What they call false pleasures are to be avoided. Pride is a false pleasure. Like, say for instance that you think your appearance is more hideous than a fellow monster's. This would be a display of pride and strongly discouraged. No one is more special than another on Montopia. They strive for uniformity and that's why every monster is only seen in varying shades of gray.

War is something that is loathed by Montopians. They hate it, yet they constantly train for it perfecting their battle skills. They only go to war in self defense to repel invaders from space or to liberate monsters in other lands, who are oppressed by larger, more powerful monsters.

Michael McGan

In conclusion, Montopia is a place where no monster owns anything and yet they own everything. Free from the pressures of trying to be the most terrible monster on the planet, they can relax and be themselves. It is a most wonderful society of monsters and a model for all."

"Whew! That was some description, Hythlodan. I'd like to talk some more about this. Perhaps pose some questions for the sake of argument, but I can see that you are weary. You should get some rest and we'll talk again tomorrow."

"Yes, you are right Moreiga. And so, I bid you both a good night." (Hythlodan stomps off, shaking the earth with each step.)

"That place sounds pretty boring to me there, Moreiga."

"You know it Gilethra, old buddy. Hey, I hear a new guy, Monster X and his gang are moving in on our turf over in Mega City, and really tearing the place up."

"What? They can't do that! Mega City is ours to tear up!"

"What do you say we go over there and kick some monster butt?"

Moreiga plods mightily off, throwing jabs in the air. Gilethra is flying menacingly by his side, smoke billowing from somewhere.

Fleeting Thoughts

IF I'M NOT OUT IN TEN MINUTES...

I was sitting in front of a shoe store waiting for it to open so I could exchange some shoes for my wife. Women love shoes. It was a fine spring morning as I sat on that bench under a *faux* tree watching the clouds through the skylights drifting slowly by like they had nowhere in particular to go. Suddenly a man and a woman walked briskly by, at a speed which would indicate that they *did* have somewhere in particular to go. But they didn't really. They were just "mall walkers".

The mall walkers are like ghostly apparitions who go around and around the mall in a trance like state. They are the undead of shoppers. They are restless spirits, stuck between being inside the stores, and being home at peace. Their hollow footsteps resound in the caverns of the mall. I'm not a mall person. I hate shopping, period. Even on those rare occasions when I have money in my pocket and I know what I'm there to buy, I feel like I'm trapped in some bizarre and surreal dream. The Mall. Let's say I'm there to buy a pair of jeans because my favorite pair has experienced a blowout in the area known as the crotch. I can never get a pair of jeans with commitment.

My love affair with my jeans is always nipped in the bud, or the knee, or the pocket, before we can reflect on the good times we've had together. So there

Michael McGan

I am in the mall with a new pair in my sweaty hands, getting dizzy, and feeling like I have to go to the bathroom. I asked myself if I wanted to spend that much money. I won't even try them on. I just find my brand, model and size, pay up and rush out feeling like I just got over the flu.

They say there's a lot of fish in the sea, well there's a lot of jeans at the mall, and who knew there were so many shades of blue? All the way home I'm thinking that I spent too much money on this new and iffy relationship, and I'll just end up in the end feeling cheated and exposed.

I'm also wondering if Levi Strauss could have envisioned all of this when he designed the once "heavy denim trousers". They're not very heavy these days, and anybody who still calls them "trousers" has probably lived through the depression and does not wear them anymore. Especially if they look at the price tags.

So I'm driving home, observing the speed limit, and I approach this red light. The woman behind me is obviously thinking I should run it, with herself in her minivan two feet from my bumper. As I listened to her screeching tires, and waited to be smashed into the next zip code, I was thinking that here is a woman in a hurry. I have a exude a protective aura around me, because she skidded around me on the left, narrowly missing me.

Now I began to think that even driving home from the mall is a stressful experience. I should have

Fleeting Thoughts

known these new jeans would be nothing but trouble for me. Maybe the lady here was one of the restless mall walking spirits who somehow broke out and came speeding back to life. My mind started to pose questions. Who is more alive, the shopper, or the person who has stayed at home? Is the bright light at the end of the tunnel the storefront, as the power is turned on and the metal gate goes up, or is it the exit leading to the sunlit parking lot?

I will leave these things for you to ponder—if you dare. As for me, I have a pair of shoes to deliver, and the slowly drifting clouds are looking much better from here. I guess they had somewhere to go after all.

Michael McGan

LOOSE CHANGE

I don't know when it actually happens, but somewhere along the way you come to the point where you stop picking up pennies that you see on the ground. It's kind of a sad thing isn't it? The penny is all dirty and worn, saying, "Pick me up! Please, pick me up." You just look down and say, "No, you're basically worthless. And besides, I might throw my back out, and for what?"

So you leave it and turn away. There's only one thing I can think of that a penny is good for, throwing it in a fountain and making a wish. We hope that the worthless penny will reproduce for us in some way.

Now I don't want to get all religious here, but I sometimes wonder if that's how God feels when He looks down on us and we're all down and out, saying, "Pick me up! Please, pick me up." He could say, "No, I'm loaded with saints and martyrs up here. You're basically worthless. And besides, I might throw my back out, and for what?"

But He picks us up and hopes we earn some interest for Him. And you know, even though He might think about it, He doesn't even throw us in a fountain, which is kind of nice. He just saves us.

Fleeting Thoughts

THE SQUEAKY WHEEL FALLS OFF

There's an old expression that says, "Use it or lose it!" This applies to many things besides the obvious one you're thinking of - perishable foods. I'm thinking more along the lines of our brain here. We have to use it or we could potentially lose it. Perhaps one of the first signs of losing it is when you're sitting there watching Bugs Bunny with your kid and saying to yourself, "He's a clever guy. I wish I could be that clever." But then again, if you have kids, your brain has an official and sanctioned leave of absence for a few years. Don't worry, you'll be back. And all those frightening images of Barney, Pokeman, The Teletubbies, etc. will eventually fade away.

We're awake for maybe sixteen or more hours a day right? Our brains are in the "on" position for that whole period of time. At the end of the day when you're lying in bed you say to yourself, "What did I think about today? How did I challenge my mind?" You can't remember. There was something about a sandwich, and maybe something about your boss, something going on next week at your kid's school, and then you pass out. Although your brain is now in the "off" position, this does not necessarily mean that all thought activity is over. This is when the maid comes in to clean the place. Well alright, sometimes it might be the French maid, but you're not guilty of anything you do in a dream. (Are you?)

Sorry, I had to take a nap there. Where was I? Oh yes. So I guess we have to take our brains to the gym. We need to bulk up our wimpy gray matter. The reasoning behind this theory is that the more we use our brains, the more fit they will become. I feel that they will just get tired and shut down. Thus the nap. But who am I? The experts say that we have to exert our mental muscles, and they're a lot smarter than us. That's why they're experts, and we are not.

So there we are in the brain gym starting at the crossword pull down machine. Crosswords are good for retaining your memory. The words are hard so we ask for a spot. "Come on! You got it! Push! Push! It's all you! Eight letter word for salad ingredient, come on!" "TOMATOES!" Excellent. You might have a headache later but remember, no pain-no gain! Now we're feeling pretty good. We're looking in the mirror, doing some mental flexing, posing deep questions. Then we move on to another challenge only to find that all the machines are being used. We don't want to go over in the free weight area where the big boys are hefting consequentialist theories and stuff that would put us in the hospital. Right? I didn't think so.

So we wait around, go to the water cooler, flip through an issue of Mental Heath and Fitness, until we're totally distracted and lose that pump. Pretty soon we're thinking, "That's enough for one day. I don't want to strain anything." We get out of there, go home, turn on the tube, and watch syndicated reruns of the Love Boat. This is known as the recovery and growth period.

I recently read an article about this study, in which it is stated that people with small heads are likely to have impaired thinking ability later in life. People with large heads will be OK. I have a smallish head, which makes this very interesting. I know people with heads that are larger than life, so what does this mean? That some day they will be having some laughs at my expense as they ask me questions about physics? They can't even spell physics. Maybe I'll just whack them with my cane. Those big old pumpkin heads of theirs will make easy targets.

I wonder if the reason for this belief is that you gather all these thoughts, all this information all your life, and here you are with this small head with no more room. It's crowded, noisy, chaotic, nobody can get into the bathroom. You've got the "No Vacancy" sign out. Information is driving by, going down the road looking for a big half empty head. I don't know.

They say that getting lots of sleep can help you keep a youthful appearance. But as you get older you need less sleep. So maybe if at around forty, you start taking sleeping pills every night to give you an extra three or four hours sleep, you could beat this aging thing, right? So your sleeping all the time and some day you say to yourself, "What the hell have I done with my life? I feel like I've missed so much. But you know I look pretty good."

Then you die and everyone comes to your wake and says, "I never saw him around, was he sick?" "No, he just slept alot." "He looks good though doesn't he?" "He could pass for forty!" "Look at him. It's like he's just sleeping."

You know something is wrong when the moment of the day that you most look forward to is when you climb into bed. You can talk to your mate, or if you're not involved with anyone you can talk to yourself. Of course you could do this all day but now it's a private thing. It's the privacy. The quiet. You are now officially unavailable to the rest of the world.

You can read a book or a magazine. This is the only time of day that you might be able to absorb information without having your train of thought derailed. The only problem is your probably too tired to get anything out of your effort. The next day you'll be saying, "Yeah, I was reading something about that last night. I can't remember what it was they said about it but it looked kind of interesting."

It's funny how the magazine that the other person is reading always looks better. They're chuckling,

Fleeting Thoughts

going "hmmm", and generally seem to be enjoying theirs much more than you're enjoying yours. There's things on the cover like, "How To Have A Love Life That Will Put You In The Hospital", "How To Make An Easy Million", "How To Get What You Want From Life And Have It Delivered To Your Door Tomorrow". Your magazine cover has stuff like, ""You Better Start Saving", "How To Whip That Gut", and "The Comeback Of The Plague". So you just wait until they fall asleep, and you grab theirs. Seconds later, you too are sleeping. With the magazine on your face.

Yes, this is the the time of serenity. You are buffered from kids, pets, phone calls, and unfinished home improvement projects. Unless of course the unfinished room is your bedroom. Hunks of falling plaster from the ceiling, hitting you while you're lying there can be stimulating for the part of your brain that handles math. You think of the cost of the ceiling repair, then this leads to the cost of other repairs, then bills in general, until you see nothing but dollar bills in large denominations, jumping over a fence. You try counting them. After several thousand, you declare bankruptcy and go to sleep.

The thing is, tomorrow is a whole new day. We'll be waking up to opportunity, promise, hope, new things to learn. So every night is kind of like Christmas Eve, only when we wake up, there's no presents, or candy canes, or eggnog, or much joy in the world for that matter. Come to think of it, it's just another stinking day. Oh well, at least we have bed time to look forward to.

Fleeting Thoughts

THE COIN
(A Short Story)

A man sits woefully at a bar longing for days gone by. Or maybe just some pretzels. From the speakers comes Celtic music, instrumental, haunting, and seeming to speak of things unfinished. The man, let's say his name is James, glances up at an enormous collection of beer bottles above the bar. He notices one in particular that seems very different. He becomes fixed upon this bottle, as if it is trying to tell him something.

James asks the bartender if he could see it for a moment. Standing on a stool, the bartender takes down the bottle and hands it to James. "Don't know what to make of this one." he says and walks away. Unlike the others, there is no label, but there is something etched in what appears to be Gaelic on the bottle itself. He stares at it, feeling suddenly uneasy as there seems to be a faint silver glow from inside. There is a cork in the bottle, which strikes James as being very odd. A cork in a beer bottle?

He pulls out the cork and peeks down the neck of the bottle, not really seeing anything. He puts it to his nose and sniffs, but notices no remarkable scent. Looking inside again he sees through the silver mist, that there is a date on the bottom. Nineteen seventy five. James speaks out loud that he wishes he could return to that year in time, do things differently. Maybe change all those photos where he's wearing that tacky leisure suit.

A man in a long black coat suddenly appears next to him. "I'm here to grant your wish."

"Yeah right. What are you a genie?" James replies, looking over this stranger with the black coat and long silver hair.

"No, I'm not a genie. And I wasn't in that bottle if that's what you're thinking. That would be something!"

"Then I guess I'm not going anywhere am I?." James replies with a smile.

"Hold out your hand." the stranger calmly commands. James cautiously puts forth his hand, and a silver coin is placed in it. "If you wish to return to this present time, throw it in the sea." the man says.

"I *am* in the present time." James says sarcastically.

"Yes," says the stranger. "But not for long."

The mysterious man turns and walks away. James watches the door close behind him and for some reason now feels his strength and conscious thought flowing from his body. He puts his head down on the bar and falls fast asleep.

He awakens in a familiar old Chevy on a familiar street, in front of a familiar house. The sun is setting and the air is warm. He is a bit confused, a bit disoriented, and quite a bit younger he discovers glancing in the rear-view mirror. But it starts to come

Fleeting Thoughts

to him. "The bottle! The man in the black coat!" he barely remembers, suddenly shaking with nervous awareness. "What do I do?" he wonders outloud. What indeed.

At this time a young girl of seventeen runs to the passenger door of the car and jumps in. "Hey! What are you doing? Fallin' asleep on me out here?"

She is beautiful, he thinks to himself. Lisa, the only person he ever *really* loved. "I don't know", he manages, "I guess I did."

"Come on, we're going to miss the first movie." she says.

"Where were we going again?" he asks.

"To the drive-ins. Remember?" He doesn't, but he always did have a bad memory.

Later, during intermission, James figures he had better put his first piece of business in motion. "Lisa, I've been thinking. I feel that you should go off to that dance school like you've talked about. I think if you don't, you'll always regret it."

"Do you mean that? What about us? Would you wait for me?"

"Yes, I will wait for you. You know, I never could figure out what I wanted life to be like. I think if we hadn't broken up, you would have went off and did this when you graduated."

"What are you talking about? Broken up?"

James suddenly realizing his mistake, tries to explain it away. "It was... a dream I had! Crazy huh?"

And so it went, one after another, James tried to steer everyone in his circle to a better life. Family and friends he cautioned and coached on everything from health to career choices, never realizing that he was making profound changes. Mostly in that they began to think he was nuts and just plain started to wonder about him.

After his return, James remembering that he was enrolled in college, became passionate about his studies. The first time around he had dropped out. Now he was back, studying banking and finance, deciding to stick with it and to excel. Lisa did go off to study dance and after a while their relationship was disappearing once again. James would be late returning her calls and letters, if he returned them at all. If she traveled to see him, he could not be found. It wasn't that he didn't love Lisa. James was just James. Again. He claimed he didn't have time right now. Time is a funny thing.

James became successful in his field and made a bit of money on some stock information that he had somehow retained. Lisa danced in Broadway musicals, and went on to travel the country in a dance troupe. Soon James became obsessed with wealth and power. Money was becoming his new love. He did not try to connect with Lisa. In fact he now intentionally avoided all contact with her. He believed that getting rich came first. For all practical purposes, it was over between them. They had drifted apart.

Fleeting Thoughts

As the years slipped by he finally began to question his prosperous new life - his choices. One day he took a vacation to try and sort things out. He could not explain this nagging feeling, and even though he was standing on the deck of a lavish cruise ship, he felt as though he was perhaps not as well off as he appeared to be. He watched the sun begin to set and felt empty. He reached in his jacket pocket and pulled out a silver coin. The memory of it's origin was getting harder to recall, harder to believe. Was it all a stupid dream?

Just then, a woman came on the deck. She slowly and cautiously approached him. She was one of the dancers from the show he did not care enough to see tonight. It was Lisa.

"Can't get enough of that stuff, can you? she said, tears welling in her eyes. "I wish I could be that important to you."

James was stunned. His mind was reeling. In a flash it all made sense. She was the real reason for his return. He had been given a second chance. He wanted to come back to undue his mistakes, right the wrongs he felt he had done, and he did it all over again. Even worse. He is disgusted with himself and can barely look at her. She is so beautiful, he thinks to himself. What is wrong with me?

"Please forgive me. I know how that must sound, but...I'm so sorry for just ending things like I did." he tells her with absolute conviction. "I got caught up in things and let too much get between us. I thought there would be time...I've been such an ass, and you didn't deserve this." She stares silently at him for what seems like years. "You have no idea how you've hurt me. You're such a jerk. But you're forgiven." she says through her tears.

"Lisa, is it too late?" he asks.

"No, I don't go on for another five minutes" she answers smiling. "Like my costume?" Before he can answer, the ship suddenly lurches, and Lisa loses her balance and stumbles into him.

Catching her, he doesn't even notice that the silver coin has fallen from his hand and over the rail. He is holding her again. It's as though he has never held anything so valuable, so precious. Now he understands. The ship levels out, and as they simultaneously speak the words "I love you", neither one hears the tiny splash.

Fleeting Thoughts

OPERATION BLUE LIGHT

My mom is the greatest shopper in the world. I don't know how she does it. She knows where all the sales are going to be, on what day, when they open, how to get past the manager first thing in the morning, posing as a new clerk so she can beat the crowds. She gets in, gets results, and gets out. I think she subscribes to *The Shopper's Intelligence Weekly Report*. Entire chains of department stores have had their sales policies secretively influenced and altered by this woman.

After finding a two hundred dollar jacket that she liked, she ended up getting it for thirty-one dollars. At another store she got five pair of new shoes for fourteen dollars. She gets senior discounts on the sale discounts and more discounts from the Secret Book of Hidden Discounts that she carries. She is the master of the discount.

People in the stores probably hate to see her coming. I think they're at the point where they just leave a cup by the register and ask her to leave whatever sum she feels is appropriate. It's easier than matching wits with her and in the end, an exhausted and defeated staff bending to her will.

Nothing stops her from the sale. To my knowledge she has only had one aborted mission when she lost both shoes in mud a foot deep trying to take a shortcut over one of those islands in a mall

Michael McGan

parking lot. She fished around trying to find them for a while, but to no avail. Now with her arms as muddy as her legs, she drove home dirty, embarrassed and shoeless, vowed to fight on! The next day she was right back out there. Probably at the shoe store, doing what she does best - beating the sale.

BALCONY SEATS

The image of a choirboy is that of a squeaky clean little angel. But I was a choirboy once and I tell you that this is all terribly wrong. It was non stop temptation up there in that choirloft. We were chewing gum, passing gas, pushing and shoving, and horsing around like you wouldn't believe. Down below, the person with the best view of anything up in the choirloft was the priest on the alter, and we would just wait until he had his back to us.

We were supposed to inspire the congregation below with our young and innocent voices. They were mostly inspired to turn and look straight up trying to see who was hitting them with little wads of paper, which I'm saddened to admit were from the pages of the hymnals. Occasionally it would be the whole hymnal as someone in the front row would suddenly lose their grasp of the music, and it would *accidentally* fall over the railing. The commotion below, and the joyous muffled laughter of fellow warblers was truly a heavenly experience. Also from up there you could easily check out all the hot girls down below.

When we actually sang, the big thrills were from singing off key and changing the words, especially any songs in Latin which left plenty of room for creative interpretation. But all this had to be done subtly, selectively. If every one of us did these things at the same time, we'd all have been singing a different tune in front of angry people dressed in black robes. I guess we didn't take our singing seriously because we were Catholics, not Baptists or somebody who takes their singing very seriously. In my opinion, the worst singers are Presbyterians, but that's just *my* opinion.

By and large, Catholic congregations are not a good bunch of singers. They're always too busy looking at their watches to see if mass is going to run beyond thirty minutes, which seems to be the unspoken time frame of tolerance, especially if it's a late afternoon mass. After the sermon and communion, some of the faithful can be spotted slipping out the door heading back to the pubs and grills for what's left of happy hour. Bless their thirsty souls. Anyway, in spite of these things, Catholics are very devout, and can manifest guilt better than any other denomination.

Our musical director and organist was pretty good but would occasionally hit a bum note that would further lift our spirits. She was too busy playing the keyboards to see a lot of what was going on around her. Sometimes she'd get all whipped up into a musical frenzy, the music would speed up, we'd be figgiting, the congregation would be checking their watches, the whole scene would get frantic.

I suppose we should have been more mature, but come on. It's so hard sometimes. Especially when you're that age and expected to behave perfectly in a

Fleeting Thoughts

given situation. A serious situation. But you'd be thinking silly, crazy thoughts. It was the fact that it was the wrong time that made it the right time for these thoughts. God understands. I hope.

So, I don't know that we were anything like the Vienna Boy's Choir as far as sound quality or even self control, but at least we didn't have to give up any essential body parts just to sing. Oh my GOD!

Michael McGan

LOW VISIBILITY

If there's one thing in life that you can be sure of, it's that you can't be sure of anything. Just when it starts to look like things are starting to make sense, you throw up your hands and say, "What's the sense?" Everything is up in the air, but as the saying goes, "What goes up, must come down."

I guess we have to plan things despite the pure chance of it all. If we have a strong enough grip on the wheel of that big sailing ship our chances of getting from point A to point B are a little better overall. To continue with this metaphor, sometimes we can't get the ship out of the harbor because there is no wind to fill our sails, and the crew has gone back ashore to swill ale and wink at "Mandy, the serving wench". This leaves us waiting and wondering if perhaps we should have used a small plane as the metaphor for moving along with our plans. Don't forget the parachute.

Some people just have to know if they will succeed in this journey, and what obstacles to expect, so they turn the spirits of those who have departed for guidance and the words to today's crossword puzzles. I don't understand this whole spirit thing. If the spirit of everyone who ever lived is walking around us, flying around us, whatever, it's got to be pretty congested. How can they get anywhere? When they're called upon it has to be frustrating. "C'mon.

Fleeting Thoughts

C'mon! Somebody is callin' me here, get out of my way, would ya'? Could you just let me squeeze through there? Thank you. Was that so freakin' hard?"

In one notable case, a woman named Hellena Coiffure, an ambitious entrepreneur, called upon the spirit of her uncle Herb who had been a meteorologist. She asked him what he could foresee of her plans to combine sweatshops with aerobic studios. Hellena soon became disappointed when the only thing the milky apparition would say was, "Did you see me on Doppler last week? I was that thing hovering over the Bahamas."

It's difficult to know what will happen down the road. Can we know at all? Who knows? And do we really want to know? I don't know. You know? Outside, the things that were up in the air are silently falling about. Oh no! I stepped in that again?

Michael McGan

THE BIG SHOW

Death is a frightening and mysterious thing. Nothing to clown about, unless of course you're a total Bozo. Sometimes it helps to talk about it, to give your thoughts on it, put your spin on it. For many people, death is really puzzling. They want to face death with concrete answers. Some have faced death with concrete shoes, but still had no answers. The thing about the finality of death, is pretty much the *finality* of death. But if you've made your mark in life, reached your goals, gained the love and respect of those who know you, had some good times, paved your way for the next part of the journey, you must be very tired. Despite this, having accomplished all these things must make it easier to face the inevitable. I don't know. When I get there, I'll tell you. Or not.

We constantly hear about people who meet death and for some reason, come back. Probably forgot their toothbrush or something they would need for a prolonged stay. Death has often been portrayed as an actual character as in: Death, the Grim Reaper, or the Angel of Death, all males. I find that strange. If a male gets lost he will not stop and ask directions. So what if Death forgets the way? You'll be lost, arguing with him for eternity. "I know where I'm going. I'm Death, for crying out loud! It's just a little farther. Really."

If you can talk him into pulling over and asking directions, it is here that you might convince him that

Fleeting Thoughts

you have to use the restroom, and make a break for it. Many people seem to get away. In one such case of a return from beyond, a woman who was pronounced dead on the operating table, claims that she in fact met Death, and as a last wish, suggested that they go to the New England seashore.

Supposedly, she quickly got away from him when he fell asleep under an umbrella at the beach, so she checked back into life. This was most amazing to the doctors there in the operating room, especially when there in her hand, was the sudden appearance of a steaming clam-cake!. Inspired by her new found life the woman went on to become a circus juggler.

But what is our ultimate destination? Forget the creepy escort. Where are we headed? Many people believe many things. I am in the group that believes we're given a choice of two destinations. But first, we will stand before the big G. He will then plug in the video of our particular lives, on this incredible DVD system. It will be a condensed version though with all the mundane existence stuff edited out. It will highlight our personal best and that other stuff. Did we follow His script, or did we adlib?

When it's over, the credits will roll and we'll be told to pick up that empty Raisinettes box we kicked under the seat. Then comes the review by the ultimate critic. Many will wish there was a second feature at this point. At least a couple cartoons to buy more time. Anything but judgment.

Michael McGan

Some will wish they could return to their life and remake their movie. Maybe a few less car chases, steamy love scenes, Kung-Fu fight sequences. Whatever they wish at that point will not matter because it's a done deal. It's in the can. No remake. "If only I acted better" might be a phrase heard here. Bingo! It's time to hear where your final destination will be.

You may see it all quite differently. No one really knows if they will have an escort or what to expect at the end of that tunnel. We all just have to try and remember to keep a pair of sun glasses on us at all times. They say the lights there are pretty bright. Must be on-high beams.

Fleeting Thoughts

AN EVENING WITH BAGWEENI

Following are excerpts from a question and answer session at UCLA featuring the great Eastern philosopher and Eastern Conference Hopscotch Champion, Professor B. F. Bagweeni. After a long winded introduction on the subject of "Thinking, as a means to having profound thoughts", the questions from students begin

Questioner: How can we clear our minds in preparation for thinking?
Bagweeni: This is sometimes difficult to do because there are so many thoughts which are only distractions. They will knock on the door, but you must not answer. They will even jump up and down in front of the windows to your mind, waving their arms and perhaps wearing a pair of those glasses with the dangling eyeballs, trying to get your attention. You have to pull the shades or you may begin to grin, and the people around you will become uneasy.

Questioner: Is there such a thing as correct thinking?
Bagweeni: Once you use the word "correct", you become incorrect. Then, in the incorrect state, you begin to examine the correctness of the incorrectness of your beliefs on what is correct. Do you follow?

Michael McGan

Questioner: Ughh, sure. Yes, yes I can see it.
Bagweeni: Good. Next?

Questioner: Are the thought and the thinker one in the same?
Bagweeni: Yes and no. They are almost always inseparable, but occasionally one goes out for cigarettes. And while thoughts fill the thinker's head, the thinker is much better at filling out a suit.

Questioner: Why can I not rid my mind of beautiful women, and think more clearly of the universe?
Bagweeni: You must go to a higher level of thinking. I have found myself that beautiful women can take up an entire level of the brain, usually the third floor, so I try to not push that button. Although occasionally I stop in for a quick massage.

Questioner: Are you saying that we are in control of our thoughts?
Bagweeni: Not at all. We can not stop our thoughts because there is only one of us and so many of them. But why would we stop a thought from going where it wants to go? As long as they are back at a decent hour, what is the harm? If one of my thoughts wants to go to the movies, should I try to stop it? Should I forbid it? Perhaps I should just go along with my thought to the movies but insist that it pay for refreshments. For our thoughts are fleeting,

Fleeting Thoughts

frenzied things that skitter about, and are constantly late for appointments, but are we to blame? I think not.

Questioner: Teacher, what is the difference between Eastern philosophy, and Western philosophy?
Bagweeni: What is east? What is west? Only points on a compass. If our thoughts wander, as they are fond of doing, then they become lost of all direction, and we can only hope that they have packed some trail mix.

Questioner: What is the meaning of life?
Bagweeni: Does life have a meaning? Does everything mean something? Or can something mean nothing? Do you know what I mean? Of course you don't, how could you? I've lost myself in the endless riddles. But the pay is good. Next question?

Questioner: What kind of nut case dipstick are you anyway?
Bagweeni: Is this a good thing? A type of guru or something, a dipstick? If not, I do not take offense to this question because you are entitled to your opinions. But are they your opinions, or the collective opinions of everyone you've ever met in life? Can we form opinions without the influence of worldly experience? By the way, what do you think of my footwear?

Questioner: They're some ugly ass shoes. Why do you answer questions with more questions? Can't you just give an answer like I just did?

Bagweeni: Listen to me you silly things. Is not the question also the answer? They are connected, like lovers, but seldom seen together during daylight hours without wearing hats and dark glasses. Or look at it this way. Answers are like the birds that come when we have thrown out bread. Questions are the bread that we throw out there. But sometimes the birds are off eating worms, and when they finally do appear, they are not hungry and only pick. So we have to sneak up on them and...

Questioner: I think you're for the birds. Maybe we ought to throw you out there. You know, I heard that your real name is Bernie Fieldstone, and the farthest east that you've been, is New Jersey. You're just making this up as you go along, aren't you, Bernie? He's no philosopher, he's a fraud!

Bagweeni: Oh, look at the time. I must leave you now to think on these things that we have touched on today.

(Sitar music signals Bagweeni's hasty exit.)

Fleeting Thoughts

AND THEN I'D SIT AND THINK SOME MORE...

Upon going out to the mailbox on this humid summer day I noticed the ever darkening skies. I figured it was either a thunder storm approaching or those flying monkeys from the Wizard of Oz. Probably the former, but you never know. There in the stack of mail was yet another credit card invitation, which is kind of like going to Oz. You're trapped in this place that you can't get out of, and eventually you have to find your way to the Emerald City Credit Counseling Wizard and ask for a reduced payment plan. Then he flys off in his balloon, then you go out and put a new pair of red slippers on a new card.

This one was special though. It wasn't even an application, it was an acceptance form. No lengthy forms to fill out, no questions asked. I had been pre-approved! I had pre-approved status they said. I could get instant gratification and be flattered at the same time. Talk about compound interest! I am special.

Status, is the key word. This "status" that I had attained is not easily achieved, I was told. I must be really special. This was a "milestone" marking my "financial success" I was told. My excellent financial record, and my demonstration of financial responsibility had earned me all of this I was told. I guess what they meant is that I had in the past melted several cards, not by throwing water on them, but by paying them off, and ripping them up.

As I went through the rest of the mail, I noticed that in the same stack was a letter from a collection agency. They would be the flying monkeys. They told me in no uncertain terms that this particular bill must be paid now! Although this deal turned out to be a mistake on their part, I still had to laugh about this paradox of economics. Here I was supposed to be financially responsible, and yet I was set upon by a collection agency. Does anybody really know what's going on? If they only had a brain!

With the skies now black, I was going to get my dog and head for the storm cellar, but I thought, "Wait a minute! We don't have a storm cellar." It was just a thunder storm, not a twister., and I wouldn't end up in Munchkin Land. So I began to relax a bit and glanced at the dog just lying there. He doesn't get all worked up with these crazy thoughts. He just takes life minute by minute, and I thought, "If he can do it, why, oh why can't I?"

Fleeting Thoughts

TEA FOR TWO

Imagine that you are the last man or woman on Earth. Remember those science fiction movies like "The Omega Man"? Alright, he eventually had some problems with mutants or vampires, I don't recall. Maybe it was mutant-vampires. But that aside, Chaleton Heston had it pretty good for a while. Sure, he ended up being shiskabob in the final scene, but all good things come to end - eventually. That whole genre of "Last Person On Earth" films really made an impression on me. The character in these movies was not alone on an island, he was alone on a planet! The ultimate survivor.

Let's say that you get bored and decide that you want to cruise the strip. You need some wheels. You glance at your pathetic mini-van and come to the conclusion that you need a new image. Something that says "Hey, look at me!" You could drive a new car right through the showroom window, and out onto the street, engine screaming, tires squealing. That would be nice. You'd never run out of gas, if you could get the pumps to work that is.

If there is no electricity, you may be in California, not the least bit phased by any of this. For the rest of the world, if there is no power you may want to drive something to wherever it is that they make electricity then complain vehemently - indicating that you just might not pay this month's bill. Then you will probably have to go into the "plant" area where "power" is "generated" and start throwing some "switches" and pushing some "buttons" until you get some "juice". How complicated can it be? Back at the pumps when you dried up the regular you'd switch to super, then you'd go down to the next station.

Car trouble? No more auto mechanics ripping you off at the tune of fifty dollars an hour. You don't miss them. Just grab another car with a full tank of gas and head for the market because all that work making electricity and pumping gas has made you hungry.

You'd have to eat the perishable foods quick, but canned goods and products with an extended shelf life would be ongoing staples. Or you could just live on Hostess products. It's not like you'd care at this point, and nobody else will care, that's for sure. Nobody will *be there* to care. Heck, grab a bag of Cheese Doodles and some beer. Live it up! Grab some gum at the check out. Oh that's right, you don't have to check out. Ha ha ha.

You wouldn't want to live up north in the winter because then you'd have to deal with the whole heat thing, and shoveling snow. You would have to plow the roads if you wanted to go anywhere, and that could be a pain. So you'd be heading south. No traffic, you're doing a hundred, throwing gum wrappers out the window, no tolls. Then you'd arrive in some place warm and sunny, like Florida.

You take any beach front place that moves you, walk around town in your underwear. You don't care.

Fleeting Thoughts

You start dating manikins and throwing your voice, because manikins usually don't have a lot to say. Sure, you could put a nice dress on her, do her hair, put on her make-up and jewelry, in half the time it takes an actual live woman to do all this for herself, but it would still be more work than you'd care to do. The easy solution to this would be to leave a fully prepared manikin-date at every restaurant in town. That way, all you have to do is show up. And of course, prepare and serve the dinner... Simple, yet brilliant.

So you're in a pair of hiking boots, you haven't shaved in weeks... Many of you are out there saying "Works for me!", but for most of us, this is not a pretty picture. What kind of life would this be? If a man screams in an empty world, does he make a sound?

Most of these films have the leading character eventually meeting someone else, a live and attractive person who also has given up hope of any success at finding companionship. But as desperate as he or she might be, if they see you walking down the street in a pair of boxers, or a tacky, hoochy outfit, picking your nose and cramming powdered doughnuts in your mouth, you could actually strike out! So the lesson is, maintain personal hygiene, always go out smartly dressed, and mind your manners, even if you think you're alone.

What if they found this planet that was exactly like Earth and they set it up all the same. And then you won a contest to be the first one to go there and stake your claim, like the old west. Then, the ship leaves, goes back to earth, and later on you see a big fiery *poof* where Earth used to be. Now you're in trouble. But maybe another person has been secretly dropped off. Or perhaps they stowed away, like in the movies. There's *always* somebody else.

Remember that expression, "I wouldn't go out with you, if you were the last person on Earth." Well, you would be! Or they would be! Or you'd be the first *and* last person on a generic Earth. Whatever. So if you find yourself thrust into this scenario, and anything's possible, watch your step people. You never know.

YOU AIN'T NOTHIN BUT A MARTIAN

Elvis sighting! Yes, the King has been spotted again. This time at a *Burger* King In Wisconsin. Do you think that these sightings may be in small part due to the fact that there's probably about six zillion Elvis impersonators out there? No way. Forget the flying sheep, what's this all about? Elvis is still so loved today that people can't get enough. Even if it's only somebody mimicking him. Many do believe that he still walks, or more importantly, gyrates among us. They spot him everywhere, K-Mart, 7-11, Burger King, the White House... Could be wishful thinking, could be someone that resembles you know who, or it just might be the real thing we're seeing.

I wonder if he's ever been sighted in Roswell, New Mexico? Now that would be the conspiracy theory to top all others., including the one where the government says that what really crashed in Roswell was not a UFO, but a weather balloon full of test dummies. OK. I don't know what they have there, and I don't really care, but could there be a connection between UFO reports and Elvis reports? I propose that there just may be.

Creatures could have come down from let's say, Mars, and spotted Elvis or even an impersonator, took this to be what all Earthlings look and dress like and got caught up in human racial profiling. They then proceed to beam the King up, probe him, get all the physical statistics, use this information to transform thousands of Martians into hip swinging Elvis clones, drop them all over the place and bingo, you can't swing a guitar without hitting little green men in blue suede shoes.

This is just my own absurd theory mind you, but it's such a mystery. People just love a mystery. The Loch Ness Monster has been pretty quiet lately. Remember him? Maybe he got beamed up, probed, and used as a model of simple aquatic life on Earth. He'll be back, so... *loch out lassies* ! (Hee hee!) A little Scottish humor there.

Speaking of Scotland, sources claim to have sighted Elvis swiveling his hips in the Scottish highlands, attempting to play "All Shook Up" on the bagpipes. Scotland is where alien life forms have traced the origin of plaid. They still believe plaid to be some kind of linear coding, which may hold the secrets to the universe, including why Scottish men would wear those long, bushy sideburns. Elvis had long, bushy sideburns.... Very suspicious.

The aliens struggle with this mystery, and become very agitated when the subject of plaid comes up. Many people who report being abducted by aliens, claim that they were grilled repeatedly about plaid. Plaid is the thing that in the end, will cause the aliens to break their long silence, and beg *us* for explanations. Once we assure them that there's really no hidden messages in plaid, even if you turn it backwards, they'll probably just vaporize us.

Fleeting Thoughts

If Martians are behind the unexplained phenomena here on Earth, I think that they had better get their space-sucking butts back home because we're about to build Burger Kings right in their own rocky little backyards.

A scene at the drive-up window of a Martian Burger King:

"Here's your Whopper and your change, sir. Oh...And I like your sideburns."

"Thank you. Thank you very much. Viva Mars baby!"

Michael McGan

TAKE A SEAT

Going to the dentist is getting to be a little less painful these days. They seem to be getting a wee bit looser with the novacaine. Probably growing their own. Picture it: choppers flying overhead, searching. On the ground, men in white coats scurry to and fro trying to conceal their fresh crop. "Drop those syringes and come out with your hands up!" Novacaine madness! People slurring, dribbling, cigarettes falling out of their mouths and starting their pants on fire. It could be quite a scene.

My dentist keeps asking me if I'm alright as I lay there stiffer than a new pair of shoes, pale sweating, scenes from "The Marathon Man" running through my head. I try to tell him that I'm OK, but I have at least three hands, suction devices, drills, wads of cotton, and various unknown dental apparatus in my mouth. So my response comes out something like "Nnnnyaaaammmaarrriii." A dentist takes this as an OK to continue. You could be saying "No! I'm in serious distress here!" and they would interpret the garbled response as a signal to go ahead and fire up that drill.

I think the biggest causes of anxiety for me in the dentist chair are: (1) that I'm going to have to swallow despite the suction device, and this will cause someone's hand to move and the drill to go astray, and (2) that I don't know where my tongue is in the

Fleeting Thoughts

scheme of things, or if it will become confused and wander into harms way, like a squirrel in the road that just doesn't know which way to go, and then - Splat! Those squirrels really should be more decisive. They're so wishy-washy. Being wishy-washy is the leading cause of squirrel fatalities. You see them all over the road. "Guess he just couldn't make up his mind."

Anyway, remember when you were a kid and you'd get a lollipop or a piece of candy as you were leaving the dentist's office? You got a reward for sitting through this frightening ordeal. And you got more rotten teeth, so you could come *back* to the dentist and be terrified all over again.

They'd tell you "Never put sharp objects in your mouth. You'll ruin your teeth." and "Sugar will give you cavities." Then they go at you with metal picks, scraping and picking away, and on the way out, they hand you candy. It was all very confusing. But the point is, at the time, you got something that made it worthwhile for you. Now as an adult, all you get is a big stinking bill that scares the bejesus out of you. Makes you even more tense than when you were in that chair, then you clench and grind your teeth all the way home.

Where else would people pay these huge gobs of money to experience pain, fear, and being hopped up on a drug that leaves them numb for hours after it's all over? Don't get me wrong, dentists are not bad people. They are highly skilled professionals that provide a very important service. They give us the ability in the later stages of life, to tear into a big juicy Macintosh like a starving wolverine. Not that I've ever seen any seniors eat in this abhorrent manner...But they could if they wanted to. They wouldn't have to worry about their dentures flying across the room, and someone running for a tetanus shot and a free consultation with an attorney.

In the end, you're healthier for it all and you now have this great looking smile. But you don't feel like smiling anymore. The whole experience has caused you to become a bit traumatized. The sound of any whirling object, like those funny whistles for instance, will make you break out in a cold sweat. Your lips close so tightly together that they couldn't be pried open with a crowbar.

Your depression leads you to seek out a therapist but the experience is all too familiar. You're sitting there feeling pain, fear, and being hopped up on some drug that makes you numb. The worst part is that once again you're paying big bucks for it. I want my lollipop!

Fleeting Thoughts

COLOR MY WORLD

I was very sad when I read of yet another case of discrimination based on color. It seems that the tan and orange M&Ms have been handed their walking papers, they won't be melting in your mouth or your hands anymore. They're out, and blue is in. What's really sad about this is that ten million people actually voted on this. Half of these ten million people probably did not vote in the last presidential election. They must be tired of the same old choices. Politicians may be a lot like M&Ms, when you take off the colorful coating, aren't they all the same?

Speaking of colors, how many new colors can they add to the Crayola Crayon box before kids start needing a back-belt just to put them up on the table? There's already too many colors. Spring green, jungle green, olive green, yellow green, blue green, and your basic green. That's just the greens. Some of the colors never get used. The other crayons are down to a quarter inch, and there's copper, or apricot looking brand new. White is another one. Who needs white? The pages in the coloring book are white for cryin' out loud. Whitey is seldom called into action. He's like the Maytag repairman of the crayon box.

THE HOROSCOPES

Aries: A friend seeks you out with an interesting idea but you decide against frozen whiskey on a stick. You are a go getter. Your boss will tell you to go get donuts. You are assertive, and tell him where to go. Unemployment wont last forever. Your ambitious attitude will land you work entertaining people. OK, so it's operating the tilt-o-whirl ride at the fair, but now you'll get to do that traveling you've always wanted to do.

Taurus: You are full of bull, people will see right through your lies about being the king of a small principality, inhabited by lonely Amazon super models. A fresh start will improve your relationships. A fresh remark will get you slapped by a co-worker. Your brash and flashy style will help to open doors for you, but watch out, this could be at two thousand feet. Try not to think before you speak.

Gemini: Your persistence will pay off and a question that has nagged you will be answered. Yes, you do have an evil twin who has been soiling your reputation. Regaining control of your life will be a priority. The acceptance of your extended family returns with their silverware.

Fleeting Thoughts

Cancer: You have a knack for getting noticed, but don't go overboard. Leave the sandwich board at home this week when you go to work. Take time to relax, just be yourself. Those other identities are booked solid this week anyway. Find something good to say about everyone, even if it is a lie. Ask yourself important questions about life, but remind yourself to keep responses to three minutes or less, and don't giggle.

Leo: Strive for more dialogue with your mate, even if you must use sock puppets to convey your true feelings. Be more open to ideas and suggestions that perhaps will allow you to deal more effectively with your insistence that you are being pursued by "Iggy, the Iguana Man". Lighten up and let the world be your oyster. Don't forget your bib, as hygiene is lacking lately.

Virgo: Regrets for things you've said will disappear as your spouse is struck by a home run at the ball park. Things will go your way for a time, until they slowly begin to regain their memory. Redirect your energies into a hobby, but not the one where you dance naked around a bonfire and sing B.I.N.G.O. You will come under scrutiny. Be on your best behavior.

Libra: Dealing with others will be difficult. Throwing tantrums will relieve stress and reveal your

Michael McGan

inner child who has been pouting for some time. Cake and ice cream will heal old wounds. Music gets you moving. Your hospital stay will be short, as you trip over a hassock while doing the Frog and fracture your pelvis. Thank you cards will be in order for the kind thoughts of others.

Scorpio: Focus on the positive things in your life. No, not the results of those tests at the clinic, the other things. Smile more as this seems to make others smile. Have those missing teeth replaced while your at it. Ask yourself what you really want out of life, then ask yourself for half the rent money. Take a drive in the country, your fear of being ambushed by a herd of cattle is unfounded. Stop and smell the pastures.

Sagittarius: You are open to suggestions. You are a very relaxed person. You are getting sleepy. Whenever you hear the words, moment of silence, you will break wind. Be a risk taker. Put your best foot forward. That would be the one without that nasty fungus. Take a walk by the seashore. Your quick reflexes will come in handy when a gust of wind hurdles a beach umbrella in your direction. Catching it with your teeth is most impressive. Beach babes are in your future.

Capricorn: Move quickly to find romance, otherwise "Linda the Lizard Woman" will run off with "Freddy the Fire Eater". Get out of the circus

Fleeting Thoughts

atmosphere that has become your life. A change of scenery will be beneficial. Take a long awaited trip, but wear clean underwear. There may be a minor accident as your train leaves the tracks and plunges down a mountain gorge.

Aquarius: Pamper yourself. A trip to the beauty parlor could do the trick. Then again, maybe not. Make that two trips. Spend time with friends, but not Joy, whose unhappiness could affect you. Not to mention that annoying habit of her's where she keeps repeating the phrase, "One of these days I'm just going to explode". Distance yourself. Three or four miles should do it.

Pisces: Listening carefully is in your best interest. Disregard remarks about your involvement in an illegal chinchilla raising operation. Concentrate on the good things people say about you, like, "You're quite a piece of work Sam" or "Is that really the way you look?" Obstacles arise. Try to make good time on the wall, and watch the rope swing.

Happy Birthday: If you are born today (you probably can't read this yet, ha ha ha, just kidding) you will be feeling that you are one year older. You will communicate with others today. You will eat several times, maybe cake at some point. Make good decisions today. Inciting an insurrection in the workplace is probably not a good idea until you've had coffee.

Michael McGan

ENERGY CRISIS

The biggest thing messing up your life right now is not what you would think. Nobody knows about that. Relax. And it's not a lack of education or opportunity, not the economy, not taxes, it is the POSITION OF YOUR SOFA! I know what you're asking yourself - "Why did he use capital letters for all those words?" The answer is simply that my finger hit the caps lock key. No, the real reason you are asking yourself is - "What does the position of my sofa have to do with anything?" According to the ancient science of Feng Shui (pronounced - *Feng Shui*), it has everything to do with almost everything. All of the world's troubles can be traced directly back to poorly positioned furniture. History itself may have been written based on this phenomenon.

The biggest mistake with your sofa is not having it face the door. According to Feng Shui, this is a problem because when "Chi" enters your house, it feels as though you are ignoring it, and then messes with you.

This makes you jumpy, nervous, which affects your relationships, which affects your social interactions, which affects television programming, which affects global weather patterns and so forth. Chi is energy. This is not however, the kind of energy that will run your PC. Here again, if your computer does not face the door, allowing you to see the Chi

Fleeting Thoughts

when it enters, big mistake. Possible solutions to this problem include simply moving the computer so you sit facing the door, moving the door so it's directly in front of your computer, or moving to a new home. Most people choose the easy solution - moving to a new home. But Chi will visit them there as well. So rearranging furniture is inevitable.

Room by room, practicing good Feng Shui can make a difference. Having lots of mirrors in the kitchen is important. It makes it look like you have much more food than you actually do, which makes you feel good, which makes Chi feel good, and this goes out in a rippling effect as mentioned earlier, until the world is one big ball of positivity. That's right, positivity. It can all start right in your home. When you watch the news at night, sitting on your poorly positioned sofa picking corn chip crumbs out of your chest hair and see all the bad stuff happening, don't you feel that you should be doing something about it? Would it kill you to put a few mirrors in the kitchen? Turn your hideous sofa towards the door?

The bedroom is another area where you need to be careful. More fun with mirrors. According to Feng Shui, having a mirror near your bed is a *bad* idea because when you are asleep, your soul leaves your body and might be frightened by it's own image - there must be a lot of ugly souls out there. Get a full size poster of a sexy model or a handsome movie star, put it on the mirror before you go to bed, and keep

Michael McGan

everybody happy. I would think that doing this is helping to create good Chi. I could be wrong.

Window spaces in your home should open completely, not slide up and down or side to side where half is always closed. This divides the energy flow and makes you noncommittal. You want to improve the flow of energy through your window but can't decide whether to use the Queen Anne chair or the oak coffee table. Just make up your friggin' mind and heave it! Now your energy flow is undivided. When the authorities come to question you blame it all on your medicine cabinet whose sliding mirror gives a split image - making you unbalanced.

There's a whole lot to this Feng Shui stuff, I'm not saying that it's all a bunch of doo doo and I don't pretend to know about everything. Many people are firm believers in Feng Shui. Others, not so firm but believers non the less.

Could it be possible that my own personal trials and tribulations have been due to my totally brainless furniture arrangements? It gives me the shivers just thinking about it. As for you, get busy rearranging things if you want to be blissfully happy and disgustingly successful. Let's all do what we can to create positive Chi not only in our homes but in our hearts as well. And the next time someone gives you negative energy just yell right at them - "Hey, Feng Shui, pal!

Fleeting Thoughts

DEVELOPMENTAL ISSUES

Many of us live in the suburbs, which is not quite in the "country" and not quite in the city. It's that gray area in between where the traffic and street noises are not going to keep you up at night but you still have to buy sixty-thousand mile tires because you're going to be forced to drive your kids all over the map to somewhere they can be entertained. It's so boring where *you* live.

Their friends from school don't live around the block (there are no blocks) they live five or ten miles away in some other sprawling "development", usually with names like "Prestigious Acres" or "Gooseberry Estates" and nicer houses than yours. These developments are always "nestled" in "desirable" locations.

We live in an older, undesirable development nestled in so much sand, that for fifteen years I've been unable to grow a real lawn. The plus side is that we have little fear of flooding. "If it's green like grass, it stays." is our motto now. Being in a development, you are still very close to other homeowners who are your "neighbors". Neighbors come in all types. I have one neighbor who is always inviting me over for parties and barbecues. I have another neighbor who is also constantly inviting me over. "Why don't you come over here, so I can kick your ass!" he'll say. Sometimes I'll get both invitations on the same day, and I don't know what to do. Should I have a burger and some potato salad *before* I get my ass kicked? Do I have to wait an hour after I eat, or what? It's all so confusing.

This development was built during the late sixties and early seventies when people were wearing platform shoes and consuming large quantities of mind altering drugs. Even builders, apparently. The colors of the aluminum siding that graced these houses is solid evidence of that. Ours was bright yellow but now fading from a process called oxidation. This is where the paint forms a powder that runs all over your windows when it rains. If you have a rose colored house you would often be looking out your windows at the world through rose colored glasses. Very cheery. Our windows become more of a jaundiced yellow.

Yellow is a bright, flowery color that attracts many species of bees who are constantly trying to pollinate our house. They nest in every crack in the foundation. Every tiny opening in the soffits where birds have not already nested. Openings where aluminum has shifted or blown away during high winds. To these creatures nestled in our house, this is truly a desirable location.

We live in a "Ranch House". Ranch houses became popular out west on the prairies. They are single story houses with low roof lines, that on the prairie seems like a good idea because of the constant winds and the threat of twisters. In a wooded development in

Fleeting Thoughts

upstate New York these low roofs only serve to cause contusions, abrasions, and obscenities when you're crawling around up in the "attic", putting in insulation because it's nineteen degrees outside and insulation was not on the builder's *priority list*.

The whole "ranch" theme, complete with Western street names such as "Tumbleweed Drive", and split rail fencing that may barely contain your horses, cows and pigs, but definitely not your basic non-ranch pets such as dogs and cats, is ludicrous pardner! What were they smoking?

We are no more ranchers or settlers than we are space travelers colonizing the moon. It's a good thing the sixties and seventies are over because that would have been next - "Podular Homes". Developments would be out, "colonies" or "outposts" would be in. "Turn left on Pluto Drive, another left on Cosmos Court and the next left should put you right on Uranus."

In our development, lumber is another item that was not on the builder's priority list. The batteries would go dead in your stud-finder before you had any success at finding an actual two by four. (Yes, we're talking pre two by six construction here.) I think the standard code for distance of wall studs in something like sixteen inches on center. In our house it's all random, averaging about sixteen *feet* on center. Every time a wall was opened up for some improvement project, usually under the direction of my father-in-law (who was a legitimate builder and craftsman) several things had to be done.

First, I had to stop him from cursing and swearing he would kill the person that built this house if he ever ran into him. I was steadying a step ladder for him one day as we were installing book shelves on the wall when suddenly, in a moment of frustration, he spoke some "French" and then angrily swung his hammer down striking me in the forehead. When the stars and little animated birds cleared out I could see him struggling to stay on the ladder as he laughed so hard it brought tears to his eyes. Mine too.

Next we filled any open wall with studs, by code. Then, for doors and windows, we used real 'headers" which are massive pieces of wood that look like they were used for holding up a barn or something that would actually be found on a "ranch", and of course we used plenty of nails which seems to be another area where the builder saved big. One bedroom window we were replacing, a single pane slider, was actually being held in place by two nails. From pounding *myself* with a hammer, I had more blood blistered nails on my hands than construction nails used in this house.

And lastly we stuffed all open wall area with insulation. Lots of it. What was in the walls and ceiling was one layer, about as thick as a blueprint. Multiply the savings by a couple of hundred homes and you get the picture. El Dorados, leisure suits, and boogie nights for the builders. For you, the

Fleeting Thoughts

homeowner, years of projects and sleepless nights as joint compound from some kind of cheesy, swirling, "stucco stalactite" effect by the previous homeowner, who in a delusional moment, must have truly believed that this would be attractive, falls off the ceiling onto your head as you lay there wondering why you wouldn't listen to anybody when you were looking at houses.

My father told me that I was crazy to buy this house, that I should have bought another house that we had looked at together. He was a handyman himself and knowlegable in things that would require large doses of tools, time and money. "But this house has a bigger yard!" I would say. Looking back, I now believe that I know what both my father and my father-in-law must have thinking - "The big backyard will come in handy because if you bulldoze this house, you'll have lots of room to bury it."

Speaking of things buried in the backyard, there is a parakeet named "Pretty Bird", a hamster, a gerbil, and a dog named "Shamus" who had to be cremated because he passed in the dead of winter when burying him proved too difficult. His remains sat on our kitchen counter until spring, when we could give him a proper ceremony. I figure the kitchen counter must be pretty close to heaven for a dog. When we did get around to burying him, we didn't dump his ashes into a hole in the ground, we left him in the container so we could dig him up and take him with us when we move. He would want to be nestled in a more desirable location.

About the Author

Michael McGan is the distinguished winner of the Nobel Prize, the Pulitzer Prize, an Emmy for his work in "DISCLAIMER:", a Grammy for his hit song "NONE OF THIS IS TRUE!", and an Oscar for his brilliant performance in "I AM A BIG FAT LIAR". The truth be known, he has never won a trophy of any kind. He is just a working stiff and struggling author living in upstate New York with his wife and kids.

Printed in the United States
5716R